PUT YOUR FINANCES IN ORDER . . .

Assets . . . liabilities . . . net worth . . . income . . . expenses . . . savings . . . investments . . . debt financing . . . credit cards . . . debit cards . . . student loans . . . car loans . . . home equity loans . . . mortgages . . . buying vs. renting . . . credit reports . . . leverage . . . refinancing . . . smart banking . . . brokerage firms . . . credit unions . . . the best checking accounts . . . a quick primer on mutual fund and stock investing . . . IRAs . . . SEPs . . . 401(k)s . . . getting the best value on insurance . . . how to cut your tax bill . . . dozens of ways to cut costs and increase your bottom line

. . . AND BECOME A WINNER IN THE MONEY GAME

with this cost-cutting, wealth-building guide that you can turn to and follow with confidence your whole financial life.

The Neatest Little Guide to Personal Finance

The
Neatest Little
Guide to
Personal Finance

JASON KELLY

A PLUME BOOK

PLUME
Published by the Penguin Group
Penguin Putnam Inc., 375 Hudson Street, New York, New York 10014, U.S.A.
Penguin Books Ltd, 27 Wrights Lane, London W8 5TZ, England
Penguin Books Australia Ltd, Ringwood, Victoria, Australia
Penguin Books Canada Ltd, 10 Alcorn Avenue, Toronto, Ontario, Canada M4V 3B2
Penguin Books (N.Z.) Ltd, 182–190 Wairau Road, Auckland 10, New Zealand

Penguin Books Ltd, Registered Offices: Harmondsworth, Middlesex, England

First published by Plume, a member of Penguin Putnam Inc.

First Printing, January, 1999
10 9 8 7 6 5 4 3 2 1

 REGISTERED TRADEMARK—MARCA REGISTRADA

LIBRARY OF CONGRESS CATALOGING-IN-PUBLICATION DATA:
Kelly, Jason.
    The neatest little guide to personal finance / Jason Kelly.
      p.   cm.
    ISBN: 0-452-28061-3
    1. Finance, Personal.   I. Title.
  HG179.K446   1999
  332.024–dc21   98-38220
                                                 CIP

Printed in the United States of America
Set in Times New Roman

Acknowledgments

As my fabulous editor, Jennifer Dickerson, remarked, this is the most personal of my money books. That's fitting since it's about personal finance. It's also fitting because it took me on a tour of everything I've been taught about money and the best way to manage it.

For that I have my family to thank. My grandfather and father are frugal men who showed me the value of saving and investing. My mother is one of the best bargain hunters I've ever met—a necessary skill when raising seven children. Not only are my family members good with money, they are my chief supporters. Their affection pays a dividend more valuable than numbers on paper.

Doris Michaels is my literary agent through triumphs and travails on both sides of the continent. I'm proud to be represented by her agency. The publishing world can be tough. Good friends are hard to find. Doris is one of mine.

Another good friend of mine is Jennifer Dickerson at Plume. I can't imagine an editor who would understand my writing style better than she does. Sometimes her edits are so good that I question why I'm even necessary to these projects. I suppose I still fit in somewhere, but the guidance from Jennifer is a huge part of this series. It wouldn't be the same without her.

Ten Steps To Fixing Your Finances

1. Look at Your Money and What You Do with It   **3**

2. Create a Simple Spending Plan   **17**

3. Escape and Avoid the Bad Kind of Debt   **46**

4. Manage the Good Kind of Debt   **76**

5. Become a Smart Banking Customer   **108**

6. Begin a Neat Little Investment Program   **121**

7. Start a Retirement Program   **170**

8. Protect Your Money with Insurance   **180**

9. Cut Your Taxes   **200**

10. Teach Your Children About Money   **203**

Contents

1. Your Path to Prosperity   **1**

2. Your Money and What You Do with It   **3**

Your Current Net Worth   **3**
Assets   4
    Current Assets   4
    Investment Assets   5
    Personal Property   5
    Real Estate   6
    Add Up Your Assets   7
Liabilities   7
    Current Liabilities   8
    Loans   8
    Mortgages   9
    Add Up Your Liabilities   9
Your Net Worth   9
    If It's Less Than Your Annual Income   10
    If It's Between One and Three Years'
       Annual Income   10
    If It's More Than Three Years' Annual Income   10
    If It's More Than Five Hundred Years'
       Annual Income   11
Continue Watching Your Net Worth   11

Your Income   **12**
   Write Down Your Income   12
   Look for Ways to Earn More   12
Your Expenses   **13**
   Track Every Expense   13
   Why You Should Reduce Expenses   15
   To Get out of Debt   15
   To Keep Your Money Instead of Paying Taxes   16
   To Put Time and Good Habits on Your Side   16
   To Prepare for Emergencies   17
   To Invest for a Brighter Future   17
   The Simplest Spending Plan in History   17
      Examine Your Expenses and Find Trouble   18
      Reduce Big Expenses   19
         Housing   19
         Automobile   21
         Vacations   24
         Home Electronics   25
         Home Appliances   26
      Reduce Small Recurring Expenses   27
         Dining Out   27
         Entertainment and Recreation   29
         Telephone   31
         Clothing   33
         Holidays, Birthdays, and Gifts   34
         Gambling   35
         Banking   35
         Personal Health: Care and Fitness   36
      Keep the "Personal" in Your Finances   38
      Become a Frugal Freak   40
         Buy the Best but Buy It Once   40
         Buy in Bulk—Especially During a Sale   40
         Join a Superstore and Buy Wholesale   41
         Buy out of Season   42
      Make Trade-offs to Stay Happy   42
      Make Changes Gradually   43

Redirect Your Free Cash   **43**
    Establish an Emergency Fund   43
    Start a Regular Savings Plan   44

3. Escaping and Avoiding the Bad Kind of Debt   46

Why Debt Is Bad   **46**
    It Makes You Earn Money for Somebody Else   47
    It's Very Expensive   48
    It Grows and Grows and Grows   48
Getting Out of the Debt You're In   **49**
    Pay Your Most Expensive Debt First   49
    Consolidate into a Cheaper Loan   51
Staying Out of Debt in the Future   **53**
    Spend Less Than You Earn   53
    Convert Debt Payments into Savings   53
Use Credit Cards the Right Way   **54**
    Never Use Department Store Cards   54
    Keep No More Than Two Major Cards   55
        Find Cards with No Annual Fee   55
        Find Cards with Incentive Plans   55
    Pay Your Balance in Full for a Free Loan   57
    Consider a Debit Card Instead   58
Getting a Good Car Loan and a Cheap Price   **59**
    Conduct Thorough Research   60
    Start at a Bank or Credit Union   62
    Pay a Lot and Pay the Rest Quickly   62
    Do Not Lease   63
    Out-deal the Dealer   65
    Buy at the Right Time   66
    Consider Dealer Financing   67
    No Silly, Expensive Options   68
    Enjoy Your New Car   68
Getting a Good Home Equity Loan   **69**
    Beware the Upfront Fees   70
    Choose the Right Rate   71

Checking Your Credit Report   **71**
Bankruptcy as a Fresh Start   **72**

4. Managing the Good Kind of Debt   **76**

When Debt Works in Your Favor   **76**
Home Loans   **77**
  Whether to Buy or Rent   78
    The Cost of Owning   78
    How Long You Will Live in the Area   82
    The Opportunity Cost of Buying   83
  How Much You Can Borrow   85
    Your Income   85
    Your Long-term Debt   86
    Know Both Limits   87
  Pay a Lot and Pay the Rest Quickly   88
    Half the Time, Twice the Savings   89
    More Frequent Payments   90
    Same Amount of Money, but Faster   91
  Types of Mortgages   92
    Fixed-Rate   92
      Points   93
      Other Fees   93
    Adjustable Rate   94
      The Adjustment Formula   95
      The Adjustment Frequency   95
    Balloon Loan   95
  Choosing the Right Mortgage   96
  Choosing the Right Lender   96
  Refinancing   97
Student Loans   **98**
  Student Aid and Scholarships First   100
  Look at Cheaper Schools   102
  Use Debt-Beating Payment Strategies   103
Business Loans   **104**

5. Smart Banking — **108**

Credit Unions are Better Than Banks — **108**
How to Find and Get into One — 109
Proximity Doesn't Matter — 110
Brokerage Firms Are Better Than Banks — **111**
Get a Good Checking Account — **114**
Profile of a Good Checking Account — 114
Manage It Well — 116
Your Checkbook — 116
Automate Your Life — 117
Put the ATM on Your Side — **118**
Beware Bank Savings and Investments — **120**

6. The Neatest Little Investment Primer — 121

Prepare to Invest — **121**
What People Mean by "the Market" — 122
The Three Assets and Their Objectives — 123
Stocks for Growth — 124
Bonds for Income — 125
Money Market for Stability — 125
Comparing the Three — 125
Understanding Risk — 126
Risk and Reward — 126
Time and Risk Are Your Friends — 127
How Much Risk Is Right for You? — 129
How Much Time Do You Have? — 130
How Do You Feel About Investment Risk? — 131
How Old Are You? — 131
How Much Money Do You Have
Outside of Your Investment Goals? — 132
Choose an Acceptable Risk Level for Your Goals — 132
Mutual Funds — **132**
What Is a Mutual Fund? — 132
Open-end vs. Closed-end Funds — 134
Load vs. No-Load Funds — 134

Expense Ratios 135
Why Mutual Funds Are So Good 136
Types of Mutual Funds 137
Stock Funds 137
Large Company 137
Medium Company 138
Small Company 139
Sector 139
Bond Funds 140
Money Market Funds 140
Global and International Funds 141
Index Funds 141
Your Mutual Fund Portfolio 142
Allocating for Your Goals 143
When and How to Sell a Fund 145
Stocks **145**
Why Stocks Are Good Investments 146
Stocks Allow You to Own Successful Companies 146
Stocks Have Been the Best Investments over Time 147
How You Make Money Owning Stocks 148
Through Capital Appreciation 148
Through Dividends 148
Total Return 149
All About Stock Splits 149
Mutual Funds Are Best for Most People 150
How to Evaluate Stocks 151
Growth Investing vs. Value Investing 151
Growth Investing 151
Value Investing 153
Combining Growth and Value 154
Three Stock Classifications You Should Know 154
Company Size 155
Industry Classification 156
Growth or Value 157
Start with Name-Brand Companies 157
Buy on the Dips 158

Stay the Course 159
Ignore the Gurus 159
Forecasting or Marketing? 160
We Could All Be Gurus 161
You Knew This Was Coming, so Why Worry? 162
Your First Investment Account 162
Discount Brokerage Firms 162
Some Smart Choices 164
Reinvest Dividends 164
Dollar-Cost Average 165
Your Path to Investment Prosperity 166
Save the Minimum Amounts Needed 167
Build a Core of Mutual Funds 167
Buy Stock in Name-Brand Companies 168
Look for Buying Opportunities 168
Discover the Companies of the Future 169

7. Investing to Retire 170

Think About Retirement Now 170
Put Time on Your Side 170
Minimize Taxes 171
Benefit from Matching Contributions 172
Types of Retirement Accounts 172
Individual Retirement Accounts (IRAs) 173
Traditional 173
Roth 174
Simplified Employee Pension (SEP) 174
Choosing the Right One 175
Company Retirement Plans 175
401(k) 176
403(b) 177
Social Security 177
How Much to Invest for Retirement 178

8. All About Insurance   180

The Right Way to Handle Insurance   **180**
Premiums and Deductibles   181
Don't Waste Money on Small Items   183
Get as Much Coverage as Possible   183
Insuring What You Own   **184**
Automobile Insurance   184
The Four Types of Coverage   184
How to Save on Auto Insurance   185
Homeowner's or Renter's Insurance   186
Three Components   186
Dwelling Coverage   187
Personal Property Coverage   187
Liability Coverage   188
How to Save on Homeowner's Insurance   188
Umbrella Insurance   188
Insuring Yourself and Your Family   **189**
Health Insurance   189
Fee-for-Service and Managed Care   189
Getting the Best Value on Health Insurance   191
Consider Outpatient Clinics   192
Disability Insurance   193
How Much for How Long   193
Employer Plans   194
Individual Plans   194
How to Save on Disability Insurance   195
Life Insurance   196
Term Life Insurance   197
Permanent Life Insurance   197
How to Save on Term Life Insurance   199

9. Taxes, Toddlers, and Tools   200

Cut Your Taxes   **200**
Don't Get a Refund   200
Start a Business   201

Contribute More to Retirement 203
Stop Worrying About Audits 203
Teach Your Toddlers About Money **203**
Tools to Help You Get Ahead **204**
Banking and Credit Unions 205
Books 205
Buying a Home 205
Community Organizations 206
Credit Cards 206
Credit Reports 206
Debt 207
Discount Brokerage Firms 207
Free Mutual Fund Trading, Fairly
  Cheap Stock Trading 207
Dirt Cheap Stock Trading 207
Insurance 208
Long-distance Phone Companies 208
Mail-order Companies 209
Neatest Little Publications 209
Personal Finance Software 210
Student Loans 211
Superstores and Wholesale 212

10. Aloha! **213**

Net Worth Worksheet **214**
Monthly Expenses **216**
Yearly Expenses **218**

1 / Your Path to Prosperity

Welcome to prosperity! By following the simple advice in this guidebook you will be able to stop spending yourself into debt, begin an investment program, and create the freedom to live the life you want.

Dead-end jobs ruin your life. Working in the wrong profession ruins your life. It is not possible to lead a crummy work life and a fulfilling personal life. They're interconnected. When one is rotten, the other tastes bad as well.

When you manage your money poorly, you trap yourself into a life of indentured servitude. You do not have the freedom to quit your job in pursuit of a better one or to start your own company. You have bills to pay and you need money to pay them. So you go to work wherever you can. Years go by. You still have bills and you're still at the crummy job. You begin to hate your life. You drive an expensive car to a crummy job to make money to pay for the car to drive to a crummy job to pay the bills—you see how unhappy it can all become.

By contrast, anybody with a pile of money invested can live the life they want. If your job isn't the one you want, you leave. You calmly locate a better job on your terms, not on the terms of never-ending bills. When you find the better job, you take it. You meet friendly people. You expand your circle of friends and business associates. You make more money to add to your investments.

You may be confused by the hundreds of financial decisions facing you every month, wondering where your money goes, asking yourself every day if there isn't a happier way to get by. There is. Here is everything you need to know about money:

Spend less than you earn, invest the difference, and protect what you have.

Easy, isn't it? This book will teach you what you need to know to make that sentence govern your financial life. It will become your beacon through the fog of advertising, peer pressure, and impulsive spending. Its simplicity is its power, and your life can change by placing it foremost in your mind.

When you have read the last page I want you to set the book down, look out the window, and say, "There really is a better way. I've finally found it. I'm going to use it."

2 / Your Money and What You Do with It

Let's begin by looking at the money you have and what you do with it. This chapter will find the habits that need to change for you to keep more of what you earn. Spending less than you earn is the most important part of financial prosperity.

Your Current Net Worth

Before you start examining your earning and spending, it's a good idea to look at what you own and what you owe right now. It will give you a starting point to measure your future progress.

Your net worth is your financial assets minus your financial liabilities. An asset is anything of yours that has monetary worth, such as your bank accounts, investments, retirement plans, home, and automobiles. A liability is anything that costs you money, such as loans, credit card balances, and college debt.

After reading this book, you'll enjoy watching the assets part of your net worth far outpace the liabilities part. That's what happens when you spend less than you earn and invest the difference. See where we're heading?

I've included a net worth worksheet for you at the back of the book. In this section, I'm going to take you through its various sections one at a time. I'll use the example of my friends Michael and Susan to show how easy it is to tally the information you need to figure your net worth.

Michael and Susan are a married couple, both age thirty-four. Michael works in the computer industry and earns $30,000 a year. Susan works at a law firm, earning $32,500. Even though their income is adequate, Michael and Susan feel that they can't get ahead. You'll follow along with them throughout this book to discover why and what they can do to change their situation.

Take a moment to photocopy the worksheet from the back of the book so you can fill it in as you read. Also, grab a calculator and a pencil, then gather the following information:

- The latest statements from your bank, investment companies, and retirement plan.
- The latest statements from your credit cards, car loans, student loans, mortgages, and other debts.
- Any appraisals you have for property such as jewelry, artwork, and real estate.

Assets

Assets are the things you own. The worksheet covers four different types of assets. They are current assets, investment assets, personal property, and real estate.

Current Assets

Current assets include cash and things that can be quickly converted into cash. The money in your wallet is a current asset. So is the money in your checking account, mutual funds, and savings account. Filling in these numbers will be easy because your latest statements show everything you need.

Here's how Michael and Susan stack up:

Current Assets	Michael and Susan
Cash on hand	120
Checking accounts	2,100
Savings accounts	3,000
Short-term bank CDs	0

Current Assets	Michael and Susan
Money market accounts	1,000
Other	0
TOTAL CURRENT ASSETS	$6,220

Investment Assets

Investment assets are the financial holdings that make up your long-term portfolio. If you don't have any investments yet, don't worry. You'll start building them after you get your financial house in order.

Michael and Susan looked over their investment account statements to fill out this section of the worksheet. They were pleased to discover that they can call their 401(k) providers at any time to get retirement plan account balances. Michael also has an IRA with a mutual fund company. He couldn't find a current statement, so he called the company to get his balance.

Investment Assets	Michael and Susan
401(k) or 403(b) plans	12,500
Annuities	0
IRAs	6,000
Other retirement plans	0
Long-term CDs	0
Stocks	2,500
Stock mutual funds	5,000
Bonds	0
Bond mutual funds	3,000
Other	0
TOTAL INVESTMENT ASSETS	$29,000

Personal Property

Personal property is all the stuff you own and use every day. Things like your car, recreational vehicles, furniture, artwork, jewelry, clothing, and so on.

Ballpark figures are good enough in this section. Don't drive yourself crazy trying to find the value of your particle board bookshelf. You're just trying to get a rough idea of what you own.

Michael and Susan did a bit of research to get accurate numbers in this section. For their two cars, Susan called the library to get their *Kelley Blue Book* values. Michael and Susan also own two snowmobiles. A quick call to a local dealer revealed their worth to be around $1,500 each. The family furniture is not worth much, so they decided to enter zero.

Susan has a diamond ring that her grandmother handed down to her. She took it to a local jeweler to have it appraised. It's worth $6,200.

Personal Property	Michael and Susan
Automobiles	14,000
Recreational vehicles	3,000
Home furnishings	0
Collectibles	0
Artwork	0
Jewelry	6,200
Other	0
TOTAL PERSONAL PROPERTY	$23,200

Real Estate

Real estate assets are the home you live in—if you own it—and your vacation homes, rental properties, and land. All that beachfront property you bought along Newport Beach. That ski lodge in Aspen. Your hideaway in Palm Springs.

Michael and Susan own their home. They don't have any additional properties or land. They could have paid for a professional appraisal of their home's value, but decided not to spend the money. Instead, Michael called a local real estate brokerage firm and asked for a comparable valuation on their home.

Meanwhile, Susan called two friends in the area who recently sold homes similar to Michael and Susan's. When all the numbers were in, Michael and Susan came up with $142,000 as a solid estimate of their home's current value.

Real Estate	Michael and Susan
Primary residence	142,000
Vacation home	0
Rental property	0
Land	0
Other	0
TOTAL REAL ESTATE	$142,000

Add Up Your Assets

The last part for the assets section of the worksheet is to simply carry forward the total value of your current assets, investment assets, personal property, and real estate. Add them together to get the total value of your assets. You may be surprised at how much you own!

Total Assets	Michael and Susan
Current assets	6,220
Investment assets	29,000
Personal property	23,200
Real estate	142,000
TOTAL ASSETS	$200,420

Liabilities

Liabilities are the things you owe. The worksheet covers three different types of liabilities. They are current liabilities, loans, and mortgages.

Current Liabilities

Current liabilities are debts due within one year such as your unpaid credit card balances and medical bills that you pay down gradually. Don't include bills that you pay monthly forever, like electricity and food.

Michael and Susan owe $1,850 on five department store cards. In addition, they owe $4,500 to major credit card companies. They are also paying off an orthodontist's bill of $2,800.

Current liabilities	Michael and Susan
Department store credit cards	1,850
Major credit cards	4,500
Medical and dental bills	2,800
Other	0
TOTAL CURRENT LIABILITIES	$9,150

Loans

Loans are debts due within one year to ten years. You might have borrowed money for your car, college degree, and home improvements.

Michael's car is paid for, but Susan called the bank and learned that the pay-off amount of her car loan is $5,300. Michael and Susan have only one additional loan. Michael opened a home equity line of credit to help finance a business idea of his several years ago. He still owes $11,400 on it.

Loans	Michael and Susan
Automobile loans	5,300
Educational loans	0
Personal loans	0
Installment contracts	0
Home equity loans	11,400
Other	0
TOTAL LOANS	$16,700

Mortgages

Mortgages are debts for property with payments that typically last more than ten years. Almost all mortgages are for a home or other real estate.

Michael and Susan have a mortgage on their home. To find the amount that he and Susan owe, Michael called their mortgage company and learned that their outstanding balance is $114,450.

Mortgages	Michael and Susan
Primary residence	114,450
Vacation home	0
Rental property	0
Other	0
TOTAL MORTGAGES	$114,450

Add Up Your Liabilities

The last part for the liabilities section of the worksheet is to simply carry forward the total owed on your current liabilities, loans, and mortgages. Add them together to get the total owed on your liabilities.

Total Liabilities	Michael and Susan
Current liabilities	9,150
Loans	16,700
Mortgages	114,450
TOTAL LIABILITIES	$140,300

Your Net Worth

Now that you have totaled your assets and liabilities, you should have a good idea where you stand. Michael and Susan subtracted their liabilities from their assets to determine their net worth.

Net Worth	Michael and Susan
Total assets	200,420
Total liabilities	140,300
NET WORTH (assets – liabilities)	$60,120

So, what does it all mean? It means you now have a better financial snapshot of yourself than the vast majority of your neighbors will ever have. In a quick glance, you can see if you're ahead or have some catching up to do. Let's look at your net worth in relation to your annual income.

If It's Less Than Your Annual Income

This is where most people stand. Even if you have a negative net worth, you're not alone. Everybody starts off with a net worth below their annual salary and many never push beyond that crucial point. You'll need to pay particular attention to spending wisely, getting out of debt, and investing.

If It's Between One and Three Years' Annual Income

This is where you start to stabilize on solid ground. Having at least a year's worth of income socked away provides you with peace of mind, knowing that you have a strong footing to brace yourself against difficult times like unemployment and medical emergencies. It's time to refine your goals. You've achieved stability, now you should consider what prosperity means to you. Then, you can adjust your spending and investing to strive toward that lifestyle.

If It's More Than Three Years' Annual Income

You are well on your way to the good life, particularly if your net worth is growing in the normal course of your financial habits. If you haven't yet defined what prosperity means to you, now would be a good time. You're at a stage when the mere accumulation of more money won't necessarily mean happiness or even a change that you'll notice. If you have five years of income invested, what's another six months' worth? It's just numbers on paper if you're not striving for something. Make sure you are on track toward something that will make you happier, make your life more meaningful, make the world better.

If It's More Than Five Hundred Years' Annual Income
You're reading the wrong book.

Continue Watching Your Net Worth

Figuring your current net worth is not just a fun exercise that you did once to humor me. You should take advantage of the work you've done in this section to help manage your money better.

One way is by developing a filing system. You just gathered all the papers you need to measure your financial state of being. Organize them into folders and place the folders in a file cabinet or box. As you get future statements from your bank, bills from your credit cards, loan papers, and so on, file them in the right place for easy reference.

At least once per year, update your net worth statement. Keeping it current will provide you with a simple way to make sure you're moving in the right direction, just as watching your weight provides a simple way to make sure you stay healthy. Just as your weight is a good indicator of your physical fitness, your net worth is a good indicator of your financial fitness.

A current net worth statement will help you make big financial decisions, such as whether you should buy a home or a new car. If you need a loan, your net worth statement will give you a head start on the loan officers who use the same information to determine whether you qualify.

It's important to never kid yourself about what debt means. With your net worth statement handy at all times, you'll know in advance exactly how much the debt will set you back and if it's worth the liability.

In chapter 3, we'll use your net worth statement to identify how much bad debt you're carrying. Then we'll figure a way to get rid of it. See? The fun never ends.

Your Net Worth Statement Will Tell You Whether You Can Buy It

Your Income

Now you know what you own and what you owe. Let's look at what you earn and possible ways to increase it.

Write Down Your Income

Income, glorious income. Paychecks, business profits, investment dividends, profitable hobbies; they are the lifeblood of our finances. They're also easy to track down because most people have far fewer sources of income than outgo.

Grab a blank sheet of paper then gather your pay stubs, business receipts, and deposits. Write down the amounts of everything you earn.

If you're employed, your gut reaction is that your paycheck is the only income you earn. But be sure to include everything on your worksheet. Seemingly small items such as the sale of old cars, payments for services you've rendered, and profits from hobbies can show areas where you might make more money.

In the next section, you'll consider nontraditional sources of income for potential moneymakers. A few hundred dollars of extra money every month turns into quite a nest egg when invested properly.

Look for Ways to Earn More

You should think about ways you can earn more money. If you are an employee, starting a business on the side will provide you with valuable tax deductions in addition to more money.

Start with your hobbies. If you enjoy collecting stamps, start a mail-order stamp club. If you like arts and crafts, make items that you can sell at fairs and shows. If you play a musical instrument, find a bustling area of town and start playing in front of a hat. If you draw, sell caricatures for $10. These types of sideline incomes are a lot of fun and can earn quite a bit of money.

If your hobbies don't turn up any promising ideas, move on to your skills. If you are a knowledgeable businessperson, consider teaching part-time at a local college. If you crunch numbers for a corporate accounting department, you could also prepare tax returns for individuals. If you work with computers all day long, maybe a part-time consulting business could add to your income. If you enjoy giving massages, buy a portable table for weekend and evening appointments. Take an inventory of your hobbies and skills, then go after something that can provide you with an enjoyable way to earn more money. If you choose the right sideline business, it

There Are So Many Ways to Make a Buck

might even turn into your primary career and provide you with years of happiness. That very thing happened to a former corporate writer I know. In fact, he wrote this book.

Your Expenses

Your income was the fun part. Now we'll look at how you spend your money each month.

Still reading? Good. Lots of people would have put the book down and lunged for another beer right about now. It's not always fun to scrutinize your spending habits. You might be afraid to see where the money goes, or you might think it's tedious to monitor your spending. But it's time well spent.

Knowing how you spend your money is crucial to long-term financial success. Just as you form the instinctive habit of looking both ways before crossing the street, you should form the unbreakable habit of spending less than you earn and investing the difference. Once you've developed the habit, smart spending becomes an automatic part of your life.

Besides, it's not as difficult to track your spending as you might think.

Track Every Expense

For at least one month, record everything you buy. Keep receipts and record the purchases when you get home. Use your checkbook register or bank statement to tally your recurring monthly bills.

I've included two simple expense worksheets in the back of the book for you to use. One is a monthly ledger, the other is a yearly overview. Photocopy the sheets and start recording. If you would like more complete worksheets, pick up a copy of *The Budget Kit* by Judy Lawrence.

Alternatively, you can use software such as Intuit *Quicken* or Microsoft *Money* to keep track of your spending. As cool as that seems and as functional as those packages have become, it's often simpler to just write the numbers down. As you rush through the kitchen on your way to Little League, you can pause at your expense ledger and jot down the lunch you bought earlier that day. The total time required is the two seconds it takes to write "$15.48" in the Food column. With software, you wouldn't have time to wait for the computer to boot up while the kids are waiting in the car. So you'd put it off. Then you'd lose the receipt or save it atop the growing pile of other receipts you didn't have time to enter. Eventually the pile gets so huge that you throw it away, grumbling something about life being too short. Nonetheless, millions of people swear by the software packages so I won't think less of you if you decide to use one.

Whatever method of tracking you choose, don't let anything get away. If it's easier for you, store receipts in a safe place and record them weekly—an especially good strategy if you use software. If you buy something but don't get a receipt for it—perhaps a hot dog or a donation in the collection plate—make a mental note of it. Or, if you think you might forget, write it down in a notebook or on the back of an ATM receipt as you go about your day.

I can't emphasize enough how important it is to record everything. Let's face it, most people aren't wondering where the money went because of their house payment. It's the same every month and rather hard to miss. It's not always the big expenses that kill, it's the little ones that sneak around innocently. As Ben Franklin said, "Beware of small expenses; a small leak will sink a great ship."

Find the small leaks. Record ATM fees, popcorn at the movies, coffee during breaks at work, highway tolls, and restaurant bills. This information will be very important when you get to the section on reducing your expenses.

Be sure to group your expenses into categories. Doing so allows you to see the big picture instead of getting caught up in penny-ante details. For instance, gasoline, oil changes, and inspection fees are all part of automobile expenses. That cup of coffee, along with lunch and groceries, is part of your food expenses. Take time to place expenses where they belong.

Find the Small Leaks

Avoid using the "miscellaneous" or "other" category to account for everything besides your home and car payments. It's an easy solution, but not very useful. How in the world do you begin reducing your "other" expenses? Nobody knows, so nobody does. Only by getting a clear picture of exactly where you spend your money will you be prepared to change your habits. That way, if you notice that you spend $80 per month on cups of gourmet coffee at your favorite bookstore, you can be on guard the next time you're browsing the shelves for other *Neatest Little Guides*.

Why You Should Reduce Expenses

You've recorded what you spend. The big question is, Would you like to spend more or less?

Most people want to spend less money. It's always seemed a great irony to me that we need to spend less money to have more money to spend on the things we really want. I'll bet you'd love to spend a million dollars—if you had it. You could buy beach-front property in Malibu. But you don't have it. Instead, if you're like most people, you have an income that doesn't seem to go far enough.

You need to reduce your expenses so you have more money to send chasing after the life you've always dreamed about. Let's take a moment to further define why you should reduce your expenses.

To Get out of Debt

When you spend more than you earn, you accumulate debt. As you will read exhaustively in chapter 3, I hate debt. It's the single biggest enemy killing the finances of most homes. It claims your income before you ever earn it, it costs huge amounts of money in the form of interest, and it grows like cancer. People who make debt payments have less money. So they borrow more money to meet life's necessities. The debt grows.

By spending less, you'll stop acquiring new debt. You'll also free up cash to pay down your existing debt.

To Keep Your Money Instead of Paying Taxes

I think Andrew Tobias put it best in his classic book, *The Only Investment Guide You'll Ever Need*. He wrote that a penny saved is two pennies earned. Why? Because of taxes. When you forgo a $30 restaurant meal in favor of a $5 meal at home, you save $25. But if you're in the 28 percent tax bracket, you would need to earn $34.72 before you took home $25. That's $9.72 for the IRS and $25 for you.

Saving money is less taxing than earning money. By lowering your expenditures, you will free up more money to save and invest.

To Put Time and Good Habits on Your Side

You've probably asked yourself, "Where has all the time gone?" You may have heard your friends talk about getting "stuck in a rut." They go to work, come home, pay bills, go to work, go shopping, pay bills, and so on. It's dreary, and at times it can seem that there is no hope of a better life.

Turn your human tendency to form habits into a strength, not a weakness. We only call habits "ruts" if they're bad ones. If they're good ones, they're strategies, tenacity, vision. Was Thomas Edison stuck in a rut when he showed up in his laboratory early every morning to search for the right filament used in the first light bulb? Of course not. He formed a beneficial habit. As time progressed steadily forward, he moved closer to his goal.

You can follow Edison's lead in your own life by just changing the way you spend your money. If you form the habit of spending less and investing more, then time will make you wealthier. With each passing day, your investments will increase in value. With each additional contribution to your investments, you will strengthen their ability to make even more money. A $10,000 investment makes more than a $100 investment. Form the right financial habits and you'll see your life change.

To Prepare for Emergencies

Notice that this section title says to prepare for emergencies, not just save for them. Lowering your expenses will gradually free up the three to six months of income that you should keep at all times in an emergency fund. The obvious benefit of having an emergency fund is that you're better able to survive emergencies from a financial standpoint. But lowering your expenses also prepares your mind for hard times.

When you reduce your expenses, you become aware of how capable you are of living on less. I mean less in the American sense of the word, which isn't very little compared to the rest of the world. In the United States, "less" means fewer nights on the town, a fuel-efficient automobile, and no more credit card balances. It does not mean starving in the streets, begging, unable to get health care. So let's keep that part in perspective and be grateful for where we live.

There are a lot of people living on a smaller income than yours. If they can do it, you can do it. Spending less teaches the important lesson of what we can live without. You may be surprised at how long that list can be. Cut back. When the tough times hit, you'll be ready with money and a mind that takes life's many wrinkles in stride. Always be prepared.

Always Be Prepared

To Invest for a Brighter Future

Last of all, you need to become an investor. It's hard to be an investor when you don't have any money to invest. It's hard to have money to invest when you've spent it all. That's why you need to reduce your expenses to free up cash to invest for a brighter future.

The five reasons in this section should provide you with plenty of motivation to reduce your expenses. Next we'll find a way to do it.

The Simplest Spending Plan in History

My grandfather used to say that the simplest spending plan is don't. He made and kept a lot of money in his lifetime, so it's worth listening to him.

As short and to-the-point as my grandfather's advice is, you might like a bit of elaboration. In this section, we're going to look over your expense worksheet for areas where you can cut back.

I take a two-tier strategy to taming expenses. The first is to examine big-ticket items for ways to save. These include housing, transportation, insurance, vacations, and so on.

The second is to examine smaller recurring purchases. These include phone bills, restaurant meals, entertainment, and similar costs.

The order of the two tiers is important. Too many people are penny wise and pound foolish, saving little bits of money with one hand while wasting huge amounts with the other.

A friend plays racquetball with me several times a month. He changed his club membership from seven days per week to only three, a move that saved him $10 per month. Meanwhile, he drives a fuel-guzzling sport utility vehicle hundreds of miles every week and carries thousands of dollars in debt on his Visa at 18 percent interest. If he switched to a fuel-efficient automobile and paid off his Visa, he would save far more than $10 per month. He could play racquetball any day of the week, save more money than he is currently saving, and be healthier from the extra racquetball games. Being healthy leads to even more savings in the form of medical bills avoided.

I don't want you to make foolish decisions like my friend made. That's why you're going to focus on big amounts first. Once those are pruned to their lowest possible levels, any savings you achieve in the small category will add to the growing pile of money available for you to invest.

Examine Your Expenses and Find Trouble

Look over the expense worksheets you filled out. Does anything surprise you? Did you know you paid that much in tax? Do your housing and automobile expenses combine to an amount greater than some villages earn in a year? Are you making more trips to the ATM than to the bathroom? That could be a sign of trouble—in more ways than one.

Now move to the smaller picture. Are dollars spent on coffee breaks adding up to enough money to put somebody through community college? How much have you spent on CDs and clothing and movies and restaurant meals and computer software? If you can't answer these questions, you don't have a thorough enough grasp of your expenses. Keep tracking them for this kind of detail. You can't fix what's wrong if you don't know what's wrong.

Once you've examined your spending patterns, ask yourself what needs to change. If there's something that you're spending too much on, highlight it. If there's something you can eliminate, highlight it.

Reduce Big Expenses

Your largest expenses are probably taxes, housing, and automobile. Savings on these three items can add up to thousands of dollars per year. Because taxes are a special topic, I discuss them separately in chapter 9. In this section, we'll look at ways to pare down other big expenses.

Housing

Spend no more than 28 percent of your monthly take home pay on rent or mortgage. That means that if you bring home $2,000 each month, your housing payments should be no more than $560.

Those of you living in places like San Francisco, Los Angeles, and New York are probably rolling on the floor at that thought. "Sure," you're thinking. "That doesn't even buy a decent sized van in this part of the world."

I know. In some parts of the country, the 28 percent rule just isn't possible. It's still a good yardstick to measure the size of your housing payments in relation to your income. If you pay less than 28 percent, you've probably got your housing expenses under control. If you pay more, it's worth looking into ways of reducing that expense. Because housing payments happen every month, even a modest reduction can add up to big savings.

For instance, moving from a $700 apartment to a $600 saves you $1,200 per year. If you invest that amount at a 10 percent rate of growth for ten years, it turns into $19,000. That's a pretty good down payment on your first home. If that seems like too long to wait for a financial benefit, then consider the $100 per month savings to be free long distance phone service and a few meals. No matter how you slice it, $100 every month is a lot of dough.

Can't find a cheaper place? Then try reducing the payment on your current residence. If you rent, discuss a cheaper payment with your landlord. Good tenants are hard to find. If you are one of the few and the proud, you have a lot of leverage. You might be able to shave $25 or $50 off your rent.

If you own your home and your mortgage is financed at a higher rate of interest than the current rates, consider refinancing. You could lower your payment while still owing the same amount of money. It'll cost you a bit upfront, but can more than pay for itself quickly. You don't need to move, find a new home, nothing. Just fill out paperwork and owe less each month.

What if you can't find a cheaper place and you can't lower the payments on your current place? Then consider getting a roommate. The first place to look is where you work. If you find a suitable roomie, the two of you would not only save on housing, you could save additional money by carpooling. Your schedules would need to be similar and you'd have to really like this person because you would be spending so much time together. But I've seen it work happily and save a lot of money.

If you own a home, consider renting out a room. You will save on your mortgage bill, your roomie will save on rent. It's great for everybody. With separate rooms, phone lines, and mail-boxes, people sharing homes can still enjoy privacy.

These roommate plans have an additional, nonfinancial benefit as well. If you find the right person, you'll make a great friend. One of the best buddies I ever had came into my life by sharing a room. We were both poor and didn't like each other at first. But we saved money, worked out a few rules, and became great friends. There's nothing like an equally cost-conscious roommate to help save money. You have somebody in your same financial situation looking for creative, cheap forms of entertainment. Some of the best times of my life happened while living with my poor roommate. Smiles and laughter don't cost a penny.

Finally, be smart about gas, electricity, trash, and water. Reduce gas and electric bills by insulating, installing efficient light bulbs, and buying efficient appliances. Reduce trash bills by recycling.

Here's a revolutionary thought. Dress warm in winter and cool in summer. Appropriate clothing doesn't cost as much as heating and air-conditioning. Keep your windows open and use fans. They're much cheaper than air-conditioning. Close the doors of rooms you're not using. Don't waste energy cooling or heating a spare bedroom and laundry closet.

Reduce water usage by only flushing your toilet every Friday. Just kidding, but you can put a brick in the toilet tank and install low-flow shower heads. You can also get rid of your water-sucking lawn and go for a stone garden. Stones use little water and they don't grow much. No more mowing expenses!

Automobile

The ubiquitous automobile, America's love affair. Well, affairs are expensive and this one is no exception.

Living in Los Angeles, I see more people waste more money on cars than any other single item. New cars are murderous to household budgets. They cost mountains of money to buy, encourage debt spending, depreciate at a horribly fast rate, and incur heavy insurance and registration fees. If you take nothing else from this chapter, at least take this: buy a fuel-efficient used car. That one decision could save you up to $5,000 every year.

You think I'm joking? To get anything that you're proud of, you need to spend more than $20,000. To get something that turns heads and makes hearts go pitter-patter, you're looking at more than $30,000. Even sport utility vehicles—the stupidest trend that has ever taken hold of major cities—cost more than $30,000 now. Why? For the four-wheel-drive brawn needed to negotiate parking lot speed bumps? Ah, that must be the reason people are willing to pay such high prices for vehicles that get less than twelve miles per gallon and look ridiculous if they ever go off-road. Smart.

Sport utes are not off-road vehicles. They're luxury cars on steroids. I grew up in Colorado's Rocky Mountains where off-road really means off-road. I can tell you first hand that nine out of ten sport utility vehicles are laughable when they leave pavement. If you drive on city streets, get a city car. If you drive on

Is This Really Needed in the City?

dirt roads, get a truck. A real truck. One that can haul firewood and plow snow and tow trailers and drop down to four low to pull a tree stump out of the ground.

You should buy a late-model used car. Too many people hear the word *used* and think of a backfiring jalopy. Re-educate yourself. Stop by the used section of a new car dealer and look at all the fine offerings. Once you've convinced yourself that not all used cars are embarrassments, get a car-buying guide from your local bookstore and start scouring the classifieds. If you don't feel comfortable going that route, then buy from the dealer. You'll pay more, but not nearly as much as you'd pay for one of the new cars.

Buying out of the paper is not that bad. With late-model cars, you're usually dealing with decent folks just like yourself. They're not fast-talking dealers. They just want a fair price on their car. Most ask a fair price to begin with and are willing to negotiate somewhat from there.

Here's a bit of motivation for you. I have purchased every car I've ever owned from the classified ads. I've always loved sports cars and decided to reward myself by purchasing one with the money I earned on my first book, *The Neatest Little Guide to Mutual Fund Investing*. I found a Mazda RX-7 for $4,000. It's powered by a fast rotary engine, has air-conditioning and a sun roof and a great stereo, looks sharp on the road, and has never suffered anything worse than a dead battery. Its insurance is cheap, it gets more than twenty miles per gallon, it's cheap to register. And I'll never make any car payments. Did you catch that? No car payments ever. Last of all, guess what I could sell the RX-7 for today? Right around the same $4,000 I paid for it. Used cars don't depreciate very much.

Had I purchased a brand spanking new RX-7, I would have paid $32,000. I would have needed a car loan with payments lasting five years. The new-car luster would have worn away as the payment schedule continued long into the future. The payments would have been more than $500 per month and the insurance another $200.

Buying the new RX-7 would have been as expensive as renting an apartment.

Even worse, buying a new car puts you in the new car frame of mind. When the five expensive years on the car loan are finished and you finally own your car, it isn't new anymore. So what do you do? Buy another new car with another high price tag and another five years of indentured servitude.

No, no, no! You'll never get ahead that way.

Douse yourself with cold water and get smart about this. You can still drive an attractive automobile without paying a lot of money and without shouldering the effects of depreciation. Paying $500 per month into an investment that returns 10 percent a year for five years would leave you with $39,000. At that point you could buy almost any new automobile with cash, or be even smarter and buy a used car and keep the remaining money invested for the future. That's how you get ahead in life. Invest now, buy later. Not buy now, pay somebody else forever.

That brings me to leasing. Never do it. You'll suffer all the disadvantages of buying a new car, with the added madness of *never* owning a vehicle.

Now you should be convinced of the merits of buying a used car. If you currently drive an expensive new car, sell it and get a comparable used car. You can redirect your old car payments into an investment program and start paying yourself instead of a lender.

If you are currently without a car, start saving a few hundred dollars every month and continue taking public transportation. Don't tell me that you can't afford the few hundred per month. How were you planning to pay the loan? When your savings has reached a few thousand dollars, begin searching the classifieds for the right type of used car.

Look for cars that are highly rated on maintenance costs and fuel efficiency. Most car-buying guides include these measurements. Check *Consumer Reports* to find suitable models, and then call any bank lending department or check the *Kelley Blue Book* for a car's fair price. Always know the fair price when you go to look at a car. Don't let emotions run the day.

Used Cars Are the Smart Choice

Once you own your car, treat it well. Stick to a maintenance schedule that changes oil every 3,000 miles and gets regular tune-ups. Keep your tires at the right pressure to maximize fuel efficiency. You'll read about getting the best deal on insurance in chapter 8.

Use the cheapest grade of unleaded gasoline. Every mechanic I've ever asked says that expensive grades do nothing for the car or its fuel efficiency. The expensive gasolines are sold only through marketing hype, just like the shiny new car you've wisely avoided by choosing a used one instead.

If you have any doubts about the merits of buying used, remember this. Every new car will one day be a used car. The question is, will it become a used car on your tab or somebody else's?

Vacations

The travel industry has convinced many people that "vacation" means luxury cruises around the world, expensive hotels on exotic shores, or private salons filled with umbrella drinks. Some vacations are that way, but not every one needs to be.

Asked whether he had traveled much, Henry David Thoreau replied, "Yes—around Concord." That's where he lived. You can adopt a similar strategy.

Sometimes, just getting away from home for a weekend is good enough. Take a walk through a nearby park or beach. Go camping two hours away and eat cold food from a tin can. Sleep under the stars. Some of my favorite vacations have been road trips with a tent, sleeping bag, a cooler of good food, and lots of great music.

Some of the Best Vacations Happen Here

Nature isn't your style? No problem. Find a pleasant bed and breakfast within driving distance. Take some good books and your loved one. Leave your troubles behind and your dollars in your accounts.

Even if you do want the high life, choose a luxury hotel within driving distance. See expensive shows and dine in posh restaurants. Just by cutting out the airfare you'll save hundreds of dollars per person.

When you do take a four-star world-class vacation far from home, do it off season. Not only will everything from airfare to hotels be cheaper, you'll also avoid crowds. Plus, this strategy of getting what you want when others least want it will prepare your mind for good investing. If everybody else goes to Maui in January, go in July. If everybody else flees Asian markets after a currency crunch, buy Asian stocks and mutual funds at half price. What works in saving money can also work in making money.

Shop around before taking a vacation. Get prices from several travel agents, negotiate your car rental rates, and compare hotel packages in your destination.

Finally, don't get fooled into thinking that the trip will be so much better if you just take home an extra suitcase full of expensive souvenirs. Your memories don't cost any extra, your photographs cost very little. You don't need to bring your destination home with you just to prove that you had a good time. Leave the tourist trinkets and $30 T-shirts for somebody else. Or buy just one.

Home Electronics

With all the whizbang gadgets available these days, people spend a lot on home electronics. As somebody who depends on a computer for every aspect of his career, I understand the desire to own the latest and greatest.

Check prices against mail-order catalogs. You're probably already inundated with catalogs. If not, order a current one from Damark (800-729-9000) to get started. I'm sure catalogs from other companies will follow soon afterward. Keep the most recent catalogs in a folder and compare retail ads in your newspaper with prices in the catalogs. You'll be prepared when it's time to make a purchase and can choose the best deal. That way, you'll never pay more than you should for a VCR, television, or stereo system. Don't forget to look at the shipping cost to make sure you're still getting the best deal.

As for computer equipment, again, compare retail with mail order. I've used many brands over the years and have never been more pleased than I am with mail-order systems. Not only are the prices reasonable, the quality is superb and the telephone support is usually top-notch. For current catalogs, call Dell at 800-999-3355, Gateway at 800-846-4208, and Micron at 800-209-9686.

Buy the Almost-Fastest Machine

Whether you purchase your computer equipment through the mail or at a store, follow a few simple guidelines to keep the price down on this purchase and to avoid being instantly outdated. First, buy the almost-fastest machine. The top of the line is much more expensive than the machine that was the fastest just three months ago. Don't get the 1000 megahertz chip, get the 900. If you're convinced that you need the 1000, don't buy it until the 1100 is released with great fanfare. For most users, computers became plenty fast years ago. Take my profession, for example. I'm a writer. The wait time happens in my head, not inside the computer. So far, I've had no luck upgrading.

Next, make sure the hardware is easily upgradable. What is a fast modem today will be a snail in one year. What is a huge hard drive today will be tiny in one year. Be sure you can swap out the old and pop in the new improved components as you need them. Notice, as you *need* them, not as the ads tell you that you should have them. If your "tiny" hard drive can still hold everything you need to put on it, there's no need to triple the size. By being able to upgrade your computer one part at a time as necessary, you postpone the very costly purchase of an entirely new system.

Once you learn your software and are able to get your work done, don't upgrade unless the new version includes a feature that you know you need. Never replace old software that works fine with new software that might not work fine. It leads to unnecessary computer headaches and learning time.

Stick with what works until it no longer works. That goes for everything, but seems especially hard for people to understand with regard to home electronics and software. You don't upgrade your car whenever a new model comes out. You don't upgrade your home whenever new models are built. Why behave differently with your electronics?

Home Appliances

The key to saving money on home appliances is buying only the ones you'll really use. How many people do you know who bought the latest bread maker or automatic mixer or hot dog machine or doughnut factory, only to box it up and stick it in the attic? If you're like me, plenty.

A good way to avoid the impulse to buy a nifty new appliance is to wait. When you see it in the store and are dying to buy, walk away. You've lived this long without it. You can at least live another day and probably for the rest of your life. When something is truly life-changing, such as the microwave oven, it doesn't go away overnight. It gets better, cheaper, and goes on sale regularly. There is no need to sprint home with the first one you see. Waiting and thinking, in almost all matters of finance and investing, is a valuable strategy.

Reduce Small Recurring Expenses

Once you've squeezed all the possible savings from your big expenses, you're ready to take the process to your small recurring expenses. I specify *recurring* because it's discouraging to cut corners on every tiny thing you purchase. If you're at an amusement park and want some cotton candy, buy some. It's not going to break your budget. Now if you go to the amusement park every weekend and buy $10 worth of cotton candy each trip, then there's reason to pay attention. You can see the spirit of this section.

Dining Out

After automobile expenses, dining out is probably the most pervasive means of financial suicide in America, particularly in big cities. There's food everywhere. It's not just for sustenance, either.

People eat socially whether they're hungry or not. When you get a morning away from work, it often begins with breakfast at a restaurant. When you want to do business with somebody, it's often over lunch. When you want some romance, it often starts with dinner. There are snacks available just about everywhere you wait; at the airport, at the movie theater, at the car wash.

Food, it seems, is here to stay. I've noticed that kids begin eating at a very early age and most keep the habit their entire lives.

Because eating is one of life's most repetitive activities,

small savings add up to big amounts in a hurry. Most people waste most of their food money dining out. Grocery stores are not nearly as deadly to personal budgeting as restaurants. So here are a few ways to cut your restaurant dining expenses.

You Eat Frequently, so Save Money Whenever Possible

Eat out less frequently. This one seems painfully obvious, yet it must be stated first because it leads to the biggest savings. To spend less money dining out, spend less time dining out. Pretty straightforward. It is especially important advice if you are the head of a large household. The price difference between eating at home and eating at a restaurant widens dramatically as you add more members to your family.

I know this one from experience. I am the oldest of seven children. I cannot remember a single time during my childhood that my entire family ate at a restaurant. Occasionally, my mother would take one or two of us for a burger during a day of shopping, but never the whole Kelly clan.

Now I live alone. There is little price savings when I eat at home. I can get a good healthy lunch for less than $3 and a good dinner for less than $5. By the time I tally up grocery ingredients and combine them into meals, the savings is minimal. I have decided that the meager savings is not worth forgoing the pleasure of getting away from my home office for food.

But notice the thought that went into the decision. Put the same amount of thought into your dining habits. If you live alone and find yourself spending only a few additional dollars a week to eat out, maybe you'll make the same decision I did and focus your cost savings on a different area. However, if you are like my mother and head up a large family, you need to pay close attention to what you spend on food. Dining out is no longer an attractive option.

Once you've determined how often you should be dining out, you should examine your habits during the quest for food. Is it possible to find cheaper restaurants for your regular meals? If so, it's worth doing. Take my previous example of $3 lunches and $5 dinners. Add another $2 for breakfast, such as a bagel and orange juice, and I've got a $10 dining day—around $300 per month. Not bad.

If the cost of each meal increases by only $1, the cost per day rises to $13 and the cost per month rises to $390. If the cost of each meal increases $2, the cost per day rises to $16 and the cost per month rises to $480. The price of the meals is still fairly inexpensive by today's standards. Few people balk at paying $7 for dinner. Yet, look at the dramatic impact on expenses. On items that repeat as often as eating, every dollar counts.

Now you've chosen a reasonable frequency for dining out and you've scoped out the cheapest restaurants. There's a simple way to make them even cheaper. Eat where you don't need to tip.

Is it really necessary to be waited on for every meal? Dine at restaurants that don't involve table service. That alone will save you from paying an additional 15 to 20 percent of the bill in tips. Notice that I'm not suggesting you stiff waiters and waitresses—having worked as one, I would never encourage that—I'm suggesting that you eat where they don't work.

Next, try to gravitate toward lower-cost items on the menu. Salads make for a cheap, healthy meal. So does soup. Get healthier and save money by changing what you order.

Here's the single most valuable restaurant bill reducer I can offer: drink water. Beverage prices are marked up higher than any other menu item. Here again, the healthy choice is the financially smart choice. Water is better for you than coffee or soda or alcohol. It also rinses your mouth cleaner after eating. And, most important to this discussion, it's free. A $1 soda with lunch every day adds $30 per month to your budget. A $2 beer for every dinner adds $60. A $1 cup of coffee every afternoon adds another $30. Drink water and invest the $120 beverage savings.

Eat out less frequently, choose cheaper restaurants with no table service, order low-cost items, and drink water. That's finance-friendly feeding.

Entertainment and Recreation

What's life without good times? It's not worth much, no matter how much you save by staying at home and feeling yourself get older. That's why we indulge in entertainment and recreation. This section will not take that away from you. But it will get you to think about having just as much fun on less money.

If you consistently find yourself spending money on the same type of entertainment, that's your first target. Remember, recurring expenses are the best ones to reduce.

For example, I see every movie in the theater. It has become extremely expensive to buy movie tickets and for a while I limited myself to one movie per weekend. But being the film buff that I am, I wasn't happy with that. The savings were dramatic but it didn't matter to me because I missed going regularly to the theater. I decided to find a cheaper way to see movies.

I checked various theaters in California to find the best frequent viewer program. I discovered plans that award points every time I go. As the points add up, I win free snacks and even free movie tickets. Some theaters also offer inexpensive matinee showings and special twilight shows between 4:00 and 6:00 P.M. at a price $1 cheaper than the matinee.

All of this adds up to serious savings for a frequent movie-goer like myself. At an average of twelve movies per month, paying full price would run me $96. At the twilight price, the monthly cost drops to $48. With a free movie each month, the price drops to $44. Plus, thanks to the point system, I get a free snack thrown in here and there. By saving so much on my regular movie watching, I can splurge here and there with a full-blown night on the town that includes a fancy meal and an evening show at full price. All this by just changing the way I do what I love to do. No pleasure denied, but lots of money saved.

You can conduct similar miracles with your chosen forms of entertainment and recreation. If you love concerts, see if you can buy tickets in bulk through a local agent. You might be able to see ten concerts for the price of eight. If you love opera, join a local society and enjoy the company of fellow enthusiasts while buying group discount tickets. If you ski, buy a season pass to your favorite resort. If you dance, join a club.

Once you've converted your existing forms of recreation into lower-cost equivalents, expand your horizons with new activities. There are plenty of free or low-cost forms of recreation available. Take up hiking or surfing or skating. Once you buy the equipment, you can go as often as you like without paying anything. Notice the added bonus that these activities are all healthy. What's good for your body is often good for your budget.

To score the ultimate coup, consider turning a recreational pastime into a source of income, not expense. If you love to fly planes, become an instructor at a local airport. If you love scuba diving, work at an aquarium or teach a certification program.

I love white-water rafting so I became a guide. Not only is it a great weekend getaway, I get paid to see some of California's finest rivers. It's almost too good to be true. I've made wonderful new friends, grown better at a skill that's important to me, introduced people to the great outdoors, and improved my bottom line.

Not a Bad Way to Make a Buck

Look over your favorite forms of entertainment and recreation. If one of them is something that other people enjoy as well, try making it an additional source of income. There's no better way to spend your free time than by making money at something you love.

Telephone

Chop your phone bill mercilessly. Limit the time you spend calling people, get rid of all the unnecessary add-ons, and stop trying to impress your friends and neighbors with every portable device invented. Let's start this phone bill reduction campaign with your long-distance service.

I've got news for you. If you're still restricting your long-distance calls to evenings and weekends, you're on the wrong plan. Flat-rate long-distance service costing ten cents per minute or less is now available from every major carrier. You can call across the country at 10:00 A.M. on Wednesday, 10:00 P.M. on Thursday, and 10:00 A.M. on Sunday for the exact same price.

Before doing anything else, call several long-distance companies for information about cheap flat-rate billing and how you can sign up. Write down the details of each plan, compare them to your habits, then choose the best one for you. You can reach AT&T at 888-928-8932, Excel at 800-875-9235, Sprint at 800-877-4646, and WorldCom at 888-926-6496.

After squaring yourself away with a cheaper long-distance plan, look at your local phone charges. If you don't make many calls, you should have a monthly billing plan that charges per call. If you make so many local calls that you are paying more than you would for flat-rate service, call your phone company and switch to the flat-rate plan. Nothing complicated about this, is there?

Next, closely scrutinize all the add-ons that were fun at first but are now just routine and expensive. That's what the phone company hopes will happen, by the way. They market the day-lights out of a nifty little feature, offer it free or cheap for a limited time, get everybody to sign up, then quietly raise the price and continue milking all the suckers who forgot that it's buried deep inside their phone bill every month. Stop being a sucker. Find the little charges that, as you know from my prior rantings about recurring expenses, add up in a hurry.

Call waiting can go. It's a rude feature anyway. If you're talking to somebody, then somebody else beeps into the conversation, the first caller feels slighted. Get cheap voice mail. You'll never buy tapes again, you won't have to listen to crummy recordings on a digital chip, and nobody calling you will ever get a busy signal. If you're on the phone, they simply roll to voice mail and you get their message later. Voice mail can cost less than $2 per month, which is usually less than call waiting. You'll also clear valuable space where your answering machine used to sit, only to be replaced by the newest $60 model every two years.

Caller ID can go. Everybody has blocked their numbers anyway. Just wait a few years. Once the whole world has resigned itself to being instantly identified when they make a phone call, the service will be free.

Don't Let Your Money Get Sucked into the Phone

Last and most important, strongly consider whether you need a beeper, portable phone, and car phone. Safety, you say? Give me a break. People have been driving without phones for more than a century now. Even the cheapest portable phone rates start at around $40 per month once you make a few phone calls because it's so convenient. Take the $40 from one month of savings and buy a flare gun at your local surplus store. Stick it in the trunk or glove box and drive knowing that you can signal help when you need it. I'm joking, but it's a lot cheaper way to feel safe when you drive.

As for beepers, only keep one if it's for business and it's absolutely necessary. It's not very fun to have one, and it stopped being hip years ago. Who are you competing with? Ten-year-olds at the mall? They all carry them. Do your budget and your peace of mind some good by tossing your beeper. With reliable voice mail, you can check messages from any phone in the world.

Most of the flash-flash, beep-beep cool gadgets are just expensive toys. It's interesting that the most successful people I know use the fewest number of gimmicky devices. A popular portable phone advertisement shows a young man closing a business deal from a sandy beach. The ad says, "What a great day at the office." People who really know how life works laugh at the ad. It's not a great day at the office, it's a crummy day at the beach.

Keep your work at work. When you're out on the town or getting away, don't take a slew of expensive devices with you to stay in touch. I promise that the world will still be there when you return. You'll be healthier for the time away, and you'll save money at the same time.

Clothing

Buy clothes before you need them. That allows you to buy out of season when they're on sale. The smart consumer buys swim suits and straw hats in January, ear muffs and mittens in July. Here again, you'll also train yourself to be a good investor with all the money you save.

Don't fill your closet with expensive accessories. Handbags, shoes, gloves, jewelry, and similar items are very expensive. You've probably already acquired more than you'll use in your lifetime. To confirm that, take some time to sort through your closet. Notice all the stuff you never use anymore. Why contribute to the pile with even more expensive clothing?

Avoid trendy items that will look silly in a year. Generally, the more conservative you keep your purchases, the longer they'll remain in style. Remember, the beautiful model is beautiful because of her figure and carefully made-up face. The clothing is not what makes her beautiful, but the stores want you to think so. You're still you, no matter what you wrap yourself in. Fashion models aren't going to pay your way through life, so ignore all the ads. Fashion be damned! Buy functional clothing and walk proud. You'll enjoy the benefit of never having your kids laugh at old photos of you and say, "Look at that stupid outfit!" Yes, bell bottoms were expensive fashion statements in their day.

When you wash your clothes, do it in cold water. It saves on energy bills and also prolongs the life of your wardrobe.

Holidays, Birthdays, and Gifts

Not to be a Scrooge about it, but gift-giving is a dangerous activity. Guilt and love can drive us to purchase expensive items. We mistake the price tag of gifts with the care behind the giving. But, of course, the price is not what matters.

Be strong when holidays and events approach. Set budgets for each person and remain steadfast. If you are from a large family, consider devising a gift exchange where each member is assigned just one other member. Such plans save families from marching into a mass grave of debt every holiday. I know some families that pay off Christmas until April of the following year—every single year!

Remember the spirit of giving when you make your own list. If everybody submits small gift lists of modestly priced items, nobody's budget will crumple up with the wrapping paper. Consider who will be forced to buy the gifts you specify. Part of your gift to your givers can be an affordable list of items that you would like to receive.

Are They Worth Four Months of Work?

Price limits are another good way to keep things fun but reasonable. Rules such as "nothing over $10" force everybody to get creative without going broke. You'd be surprised at the good presents that come your way for less than $10.

Convert some of the people on your annual gift list from presents to cards. A card with a thoughtful note inside can be more meaningful than a gift. It's also much less expensive.

Finally, consider making your gifts instead of buying them. I've long since forgotten who bought books and CDs and clothing and cologne and trinkets for me. But I still carry the handmade keychain that my younger sister made for me years ago. It's attractive and unique. She made it just for me. Her total cost was probably less than $2 in beads and cord, but the gift made a more lasting impression on me than others costing far more.

Gambling

Let me clue you into something. Gambling stocks have been great investments over the past many years. Their prices have risen like elevators of gold. Do you know what causes that to happen? Growing profits. Do you know where those growing profits come from? Your pocket, if you're a gambler.

There would be no gambling industry if the industry did not make money. Therefore, gambling is a long-term losing bet for everybody but the house. The house always wins. That definitive statement is why the stocks have performed so well and will probably continue doing so.

If you do gamble because you enjoy the recreation of it, then please set strict limits on the amount of money you spend. Las Vegas is a wonderfully cheap vacation spot—for people who can discipline themselves to keep their wallets shut most of the day. Even with all those cheap rooms and free drinks and $2 filet mignons, most people still manage to make it the most expensive vacation they'll ever take.

Don't be one of those people. This book is the start of a new day in your financial life. If you used to be a gambler, now you're an investor. Investors shudder at the odds in a gambling house. Instead of gambling at the casinos, why not buy stock in a few? The only way to win at gambling is to own the house.

Banking

It's silly to spend $5 each month on a checking account. "Oh, come on," you might think. "How important is $5 per month?"

By itself, not very important. But because you could just as easily save the $5 per month by finding an equally good checking account that is free, why not do it? More than the dollar amount, getting this granular in your quest for savings will further your mental commitment to saving money. If you're unwilling to let even $5 slip away unnecessarily, then I bet you're going to save a whole lot more money than that overall. Besides, $5 each month is $60 every year. That could buy a plane ticket to Hawaii in five years, just by finding a better bank. You'll learn a bunch of additional banking tips in chapter 5.

Also, don't buy your checks from the bank. Haven't you learned by now that they charge three times what mail-order companies charge? It's true. To prove it to yourself, ask for catalogs from Checks In The Mail (800-733-4443) and Current (800-204-2244). They sell attractive designs, some for as little as $3.95 for two hundred checks.

Personal Health: Care and Fitness

As with so many other financial issues, the affordable choice is the healthy choice. Stop smoking and drinking. It'll save money and extend your life. You'll have more time to enjoy the wealth of your investments.

The health benefits should be enough. Just in case they're not, let's look at how much you can save by telling the Marlboro Man to lasso somebody else. If you smoke a pack a day, you spend roughly $40 each month and $480 each year. If you also drink two six-packs of beer a week, you spend about $30 each month and $360 each year.

Drop both habits and you've got an extra $840 per year to invest. That's not chump change. At 10 percent annual growth for twenty years, it'll turn into $48,000. All for getting healthy.

After you've stopped smoking and drinking, find a cheap place to cut your hair. For you men, try a real barber, the kind with the spinning cylinder in front of the store. Not only do they provide the best haircuts in town, they're the cheapest. Hair salons in malls haven't figured out how to cut men's hair yet. Barbers know. So step up to the chair and talk about the front page of the paper with a guy who used to be a navy sailor. It'll run you around $7, including tip.

As for the beauty salon, I can't point you women to barber shops, but I can question whether you need the $50 touch-up every month. Only you can say for sure. However, consider that the mall salons will assign you a private hairdresser that can do a pretty darned good job for under $20. You'll also get coupons and a punch card so that your tenth cut is free. Saving $30 per month on hair care adds up to $360 per year. Now *that's* beautiful!

Unless you need it for the social reasons or special equipment, don't join a health club. Most of the exercise that you do there can be done on your own. You don't need a track to run on. You don't need a mat to do situps. You don't need expensive weight machines. You probably don't need a personal trainer.

If you do need the facilities, such as racquetball courts, find a low-cost club close to your home. I know people who drive thirty miles one way to get to just the right club. Out of curiosity, I went one time to see what was so special about the club to justify driving sixty miles round-trip several times each week. Nothing. I asked my friend why he went and the best he could come up with was that it had the best locker rooms.

You Can Get This Exercise Anywhere

Perhaps your mind can be a bit more flexible on this matter. Health club costs happen every month. They are recurring. You know the drill by now. Small savings multiply to big amounts. So shave a few bucks off the tab however you need to—that includes unnecessary mileage on your car.

Finally, be careful not to spend money on home exercise equipment that you'll never use. I've seen a Nordic Track make its way through five homes, including mine. Every weekend, I drive past yard sales filled with dusty metal exercise equipment. This year's hot way to build washboard abs will be next year's place to hang clothes. Be honest with yourself. Buying the equipment won't make you any healthier. You actually need to use it. If you're not going to, at least save yourself the expense.

I can't resist offering this perspective on fitness that was boldly printed on the T-shirt of a heavyset man eating an ice cream cone outside a health club in my neighborhood: NO PAIN, NO PAIN.

It's hard to argue with that.

Keep the "Personal" in Your Finances

You've probably heard the saying that it's not what you know, it's who you know. It's true, so here's a tip: know people.

Although the saying is usually made in reference to big business deals or celebrities, it applies even more convincingly to everyday folks and everyday finances. Most people never make multimillion-dollar deals by calling their favorite uncle. But plenty of people get cheap or free restaurant meals, dry cleaning, medical care, and airline tickets through friends and family. You can too.

It makes sense to do business with people you know. The quality is higher, the prices are usually reasonable, and you feel good about providing your friends and family with profit. It not only makes for good business, it makes for a happier life.

Nothing else comes close to the care you'll get by doing business with friends and family. Say your car breaks down. By going to the yellow pages, you'll sift through dozens of ads that all promise the same thing. You'll call people who answer the phone by growling "service." You'll try explaining the problem politely, after which they'll conclude by saying that they'll send a tow truck and conduct a thorough examination of the car, which will be $50. They'll call to let you know how much parts and labor will be on the repair.

If, however, you were able to call your brother the mechanic, things would go far differently. He would know you and the tone of his voice would instantly change when he heard your voice. He'd be sorry that your car was broken. He'd send a tow truck for free, carefully inspect the car himself, fix only what is broken, and charge you the bare minimum—possibly only enough to cover his costs.

There's no beating the care and bargains you get by keeping the "personal" in your finances.

You probably already know people who offer products or services you need. If you don't use their services, start trying to do so. Refer other business to them, making sure that the new customers mention that they heard about the business through you. That scores points and will lead to even better deals coming your way.

If your friends and family don't conduct business in the

areas you need, then expand your circle of friends. Get to know your business associates. When I first moved to Los Angeles, I didn't know any mechanics. I bounced from one greasy shop to another until finally settling at a friendly neighborhood shop. I got to know the owner, the head mechanic, and the front office personnel. They got to know me and my car. I brought lunch one day while they

Good Friends Make for Good Business

changed my oil. Now, I always get top-quality work at a reasonable price. Plus, I have a pleasant experience when getting my car worked on—something that is quite rare.

Once you start doing business with people you know, you can try bartering, which is a great way to save money. If you can offer your friends and family a product or service in trade, do it. I provide free investment advice and newsletter subscriptions to my dentist, he provides free dental care to me. We both come out ahead and the IRS doesn't get a dime.

Look over your expense worksheet. Do you see items that you buy repeatedly? If so, you probably buy them from the same places each month. Get to know the people at those places and sign up for any loyal customer programs they offer. Many of my associates are in the publishing business. That means lots of photocopies. They either know a private copy shop owner, or they have established business accounts and come to know the manager of their local Kinko's. Both routes lead to huge discounts.

Doing business with people I know has saved me thousands of dollars. I get my office furniture from a friend in that business, I know restaurant owners who offer inexpensive or free dining, I know my business bank manager and never pay fees, my newsletters are checked for legal exposure by a lawyer friend, and so on.

Naturally, you don't want to take advantage of your friends and family. You should reciprocate their kindness in some way, either through bartering, referrals, or gifts.

If you don't know many people and would like to meet more, consider joining community organizations. They are a convenient way to expand your circle of friends while doing some good for the community. To find clubs near you contact Elks, 773-477-2750, www.elks.org; Kiwanis, 800-549-2647, www.kiwanis.

org; Rotary, www.rotary.org; and Toastmasters, 714-858-8255, www.toastmasters.org. Also, check your phone book for local clubs.

Become a Frugal Freak

Aside from the specific money-saving advice above, you should adopt a frugal way of thinking about your expenditures. That way, you'll automatically do a little research before major purchases, find bargains, and insist on quality. Run every purchase you make through your frugality filter, trimming every unnecessary expense. This section covers basic money-saving habits.

Buy the Best but Buy It Once

When purchasing items that you will use for many years, buy the very best you can afford so that you don't need to buy them again. This technique saves money over the long term, yet allows you to enjoy the use of quality merchandise.

Cooking pans, cutlery, office equipment, and recreation gear are all items that fall into this category. If you've ever used a $3 kitchen knife, you know that they don't pay. They're flimsy, they dull quickly, and they break easily. Why go through life with a new $3 knife every year? Save until you can afford a decent set of knives that will last the rest of your life.

Buy in Bulk—Especially During a Sale

Almost everything is cheaper in bulk. As long as you are guaranteed to need the product and it won't spoil, it's a candidate for bulk purchases. Don't buy toilet paper four rolls at a time, buy fifty rolls. Don't buy rice in two-serving containers, buy thirty-pound bags. When you find silk boxer shorts at $2 a pair, buy twenty-five pairs. Buy envelopes five hundred at a time, computer paper by the case, and mailing labels by the thousands. Don't buy one postage stamp, buy one hundred. Just kidding— stamps are always the same price. But if you do find a place to buy 33-cent stamps for less, please give me a call!

When you find a sale, buy enough to last you until the next great bargain comes along. When you run out of necessities, you are forced to buy at the current price. Don't let the market dictate your expenses. Take advantage of price fluctuations by stocking up when things are affordable. As with other parts of smart spending, you'll be training yourself to be a good investor.

If you buy a lot of books, there's an easy way to save. Keep a list of titles that you want to buy, then buy them on the Internet. All three of the biggies—www.amazon.com, www.barnesandnoble.com, and www.borders. com—offer deep discounts that more than pay for the shipping charges. Once per month, hop on the Web and click through your list of books to buy. Of course, the library is still cheaper, but if you're going to buy new books, the Internet is the place to do it. Also, don't forget your local used bookstore for even better savings.

Books Can Strain Your Arms and Your Budget

Note that with groceries, buying perishable items in bulk works only for families. For single people, it wastes money. My mother buys six gallons of milk every time she goes to the grocery store. The family drinks it all before it goes sour. I am forced to buy milk in half-gallon increments because I can't drink fast enough to keep it from spoiling. However, I can freeze loaves of bread purchased in bulk and I can line my pantry with cans of corn. If you drink more milk than my family does, buy a cow.

Buying in bulk is smart even past the initial savings you'll realize. If you buy years' worth of products and store them, you get an edge on inflation. How, you ask? By using products that you purchased at last year's prices. If inflation is creeping along at 3 percent a year, and you buy two years' worth of canned corn, you avoid two 3-percent annual price hikes. If you also save 10 percent on the purchase price, you've saved around 16 percent on your money by just changing the way you buy corn.

Join a Superstore and Buy Wholesale

Along with buying bulk, buy wholesale. The two go together like peanut butter and jelly.

While you can find bulk discounts at nearly any store, the superstores specialize in it. Their discount prices are usually cheaper than the discount prices in regular grocery stores and retail outlets. Many of these clubs charge membership fees, but you should recoup that expense fairly quickly. To find a super-store near you, call Costco at 800-774-2678 and Sam's Club at 888-746-7726.

Also, pick up a copy of the *Wholesale by Mail Catalog*. You can find it at many bookstores and libraries.

Buy out of Season

I've mentioned this with regard to a few specific areas of saving, but it works in almost everything. You know that prices are determined by supply and demand. For most items, supply is fairly constant. That means the only factor affecting price is demand. When it's high, prices rise. When it's low, prices fall.

By planning ahead, you can purchase your goods and services when demand is low and prices are down. Buy firewood in the summer, cooling fans in the winter. See matinee movies or twilight shows. If you must buy a car from a dealer, do it on a stormy day in winter when you're the only customer of the day. It's amazing what deals you'll find when you're the only one looking.

Make Trade-offs to Stay Happy

Saving money does not mean denying yourself all forms of pleasure. Make trade-offs. I see almost every movie in theaters, but I rarely buy music CDs or go to concerts. I eat out frequently, but do so at inexpensive restaurants and usually drink water. I buy a lot of books, but spend little on clothing—my friends say that it shows.

Sitting on the floor in a cheap apartment drinking water and watching your checking account balance grow is hardly the goal we're after. You may have read some of the sections of this chapter and recoiled at the thought of trimming your expenses there. Perhaps you absolutely love your $50-per-month hair-dresser. If you must keep him or her on the job, look for other ways to save.

Every budget has room for further savings. Find the areas that are least important to you, the ones that won't leave you feeling unhappy when they are reduced or disappear altogether, and focus on them. Only you know what makes you happy.

Make Changes Gradually

To help yourself adjust to a leaner spending plan, move gradually. Don't go from ten CDs a month to none. Go to eight, then to four. Moving gradually will prove to you that saving money is possible and that it doesn't need to be painful and miserly. You increase your chances of sticking to the lower spending plan if you avoid shock and remain happy.

If your goal is to spend considerably less each month, distribute the savings plan over several months. For example, say you spend $200 each month dining out. You decide that you would like to lower that amount to $50. Spend $175 the first month, $125 the next, $100 the next, and reach your goal of $50 in the fourth month.

My grandfather was right in saying that the simplest spending plan is don't. Now you have specific ways that you can achieve that plan in different areas of your life. The savings you achieve today will turn into the freedom you desire tomorrow.

Redirect Your Free Cash

With all the money you save by boosting your income and trimming your expenses, you'll be able to take two basic steps toward prosperity. First, establish an emergency fund. Second, start a regular savings plan.

Establish an Emergency Fund

You should keep an emergency fund of three to six months' worth of expenses. This is money that you don't intend to use, but have on hand in case you are laid off, your business hits hard times, or a large unexpected expense lands in your lap.

The best place to keep emergency cash is a money market mutual fund. Money market funds earn more than bank savings accounts and they are just as liquid. That means you can get your money quickly. By calling the fund's toll-free number, you can request that a check be mailed to you immediately or that the money be directly transferred to another account. Some fund companies offer check-writing privileges to you, so you won't even need the extra step of calling to request your money. It's as accessible to you as any checking account.

Having a hefty emergency fund provides peace of mind. You won't panic as the economy fluctuates and threatens your source of income. There's no need to fear the unexpected when you're sitting on a pile of cash. Many of life's problems disappear when you throw money at them. Have money to throw.

Also, you'll be in a better position to negotiate with your employer if you have plenty of money socked away. You're no longer somebody who can get pushed around, held captive by the need for a steady paycheck. Change your thinking. Steady paychecks are available all around you. If you don't like where your current one is coming from, you'll have the ability to pay your expenses while you find a new one.

Your emergency reserves set you apart from the masses who would be homeless if they miss two paychecks. Two paychecks!

You'll know you've reached a state of financial well being when neither unexpected expenses nor unexpected fortunes change your day. The sudden expense is calmly taken care of by your reserves. The sudden fortune is calmly allocated to your investment plan. No sweat. No tantrums. No paycheck captivity or economic terrorism.

Fight money problems with money. Establish and maintain an emergency fund.

Start a Regular Savings Plan

Once you've stashed three to six months' worth of expenses, start saving money on a regular basis. Monthly transfers from your checking account to your investments are the simplest plan. They can be automated through mutual fund companies so that you don't need to sign checks or lick stamps.

Are you wondering how much to save? Most financial planning books recommend 10 percent, but I say that you should set aside even more. The 10 percent is just for your retirement. To get ahead in life before you retire, set aside another 10 percent outside your retirement accounts.

Yes, you should try to save 20 percent of your take-home pay every month. It won't be easy, and it might be impossible at first. But I'm convinced that anybody can save that amount by gradually reducing expenses and redirecting payment increases.

Saving Is Fun For the Whole Family

That, by the way, is a great strategy. Say that you currently bring home $30,000 per year. You should be setting aside at least $3,000 for your retirement. After that, you decide that you can't possibly save a penny more. Fine. You get a four percent raise this year, and then a six percent next year. Your new income is now $33,072. If you kept your expenses the same, you could redirect the entire $3,072 pay increase toward savings. You would then be saving the full 20 percent of your salary of two years ago. Of course, to save 20 percent of your current salary, you'd need to find an extra $600 somewhere.

If you're still not convinced that you can save 20 percent, find somebody who makes 20 percent less than you make and see how they live. Chances are good that their life looks very similar to yours. I'm sure they live in a similar neighborhood, probably drive a similar car, and probably wear similar clothing. So how are they getting by? The answer to that question will reveal how you can cut costs and start saving at least 20 percent of your money.

Now the question arises of what you should do with your savings. The most important step at this point is just to make them happen. I don't care if you take greenbacks and stuff them in a sock behind your headboard. If the amount of cash going into the sock is 20 percent of your take-home pay, I'm thrilled. You're ahead of the vast majority of Americans. Do whatever you need to do to get to the magic 20 percent. That's the hardest part of saving and investing.

Although the sock would work, I recommend starting a bank savings account or money market mutual fund. Either will protect your money from market fluctuation and provide a tiny bit of growth while you ramp up to better-performing investments.

In chapter 6, you'll learn how to begin your investment program.

3 / Escaping and Avoiding the Bad Kind of Debt

Carrying too much debt strains every aspect of your life. Debt builds on itself. You fall behind a small amount and need to catch up. But everyday needs don't disappear while you try to pay off the debt. So you charge expenses on credit cards, which leads to even more indebtedness.

It's credit card debt that harms most people. Consumers find it too easy to buy whatever catches their attention by sliding plastic across a counter. Beep, sign, separate the receipt, and you're the proud owner of a new item. It doesn't feel like real money.

But it is real money. Remember your net worth statement? Debt is a liability. Every dollar of debt reduces your assets by a dollar. Even if you save money every month, a faster rate of debt accumulation means you're falling behind.

This chapter explores the bad kind of debt in detail. You'll learn exactly why it's bad, how to escape it now, and how to avoid it in the future.

Why Debt Is Bad

This section might seem unnecessary to you. Everybody knows that debt is bad, right? Wrong, I've learned. If you're going to fully appreciate the urgency with which you need to combat debt, you must understand why it's bad.

It Makes You Earn Money for Somebody Else

When you accumulate debt, you owe payments every month. That means that a portion of your income is already earmarked for somebody else. If you continue spending more than you earn, you acquire more debt and the monthly payments increase. If they get big enough, you will never escape them.

You'll be in debt forever. All of your income will belong to somebody else.

That thought kept me awake at night as a kid, trembling in my bed, thinking of what it would be like to never get my allowance again. My father illustrated the evils of debt by allowing me to take an advance on my allowance for one month to buy a new baseball glove. It was the best baseball glove on the shelf, and I thought it would make me the best player in the league.

By the second week of owning the glove, I'd dropped it in the dirt, stepped on it with cleats, and gotten it wet in a sprinkler. It didn't look any better than anybody else's glove, and I didn't play any better than any of the other kids. Yet, I had three weeks without allowance in front of me to continue paying my father for the glove. I was in week two of my four-week advance plus one week of interest.

After a Saturday game, each boy coughed up his allowance to go for an ice cream. But I didn't have any allowance because it had all gone to pay back my father. I remember sitting on the sidewalk in front of the ice cream store while he and my teammates ate. I looked at my beat-up glove, the item I'd gone into debt to purchase. The joy of owning the glove was long gone, but the pain of buying it was more stinging than ever. I thought my father was the meanest man on earth.

Debt Stole My Ice Cream!

Today, I know different. The pain of missing an ice cream taught me one of life's most important financial lessons. Whether it's for a new baseball glove or a new wardrobe or a new automobile, debt kills. It forces you to keep working to pay somebody else instead of yourself.

By reining in your spending, you'll avoid going into debt. Then, all the money you earn will be your own. If you want an ice cream, you'll be able to buy it with cash and experience nothing but the pleasure of eating it.

It's Very Expensive

Some credit cards charge 22 percent a year. It's outrageous, but consumers routinely borrow money at that rate to buy items that they probably don't need.

Debt is even more expensive than the interest rate tells you. The stock market grows at an average rate of around 10 percent a year. By carrying debt, you are missing that 10 percent rate of growth. You not only pay high interest cost, you also suffer the lost opportunity of investing in the market. In fact, it's called opportunity cost.

So, if you borrow $4,000 at 22 percent interest and take five years to pay it off, you will pay a total of $6,600. That's $110 every month for sixty months. You not only lose the extra $2,600 of interest expense, you also miss out on the $8,500 you would have had by investing $110 every month for sixty months at 10 percent interest. Debt is very expensive.

It Grows and Grows and Grows

If you carry a $3,500 balance on a credit card with 18 percent interest and you make the minimum payment each month, it will take you forty years to pay down the debt. You would have paid $9,431 in interest on top of the $3,500 you owed.

Despite the goosebumps caused by that example, lots of people pay only the minimum owed on their credit cards. Meanwhile, they continue purchasing more than the minimum payment. So the example gets even worse. The $3,500 gets bigger each month.

Some people never escape.

Getting Out of the Debt You're In

The first order of business is getting out of the debt you've already acquired. You'll do that by attacking your most expensive debt first, then consolidating the remainder into a cheaper loan.

Pay Your Most Expensive Debt First

Begin by listing all of your debts on a sheet of paper. Record the interest rate associated with each of your debts. If you don't know the interest rate for certain loans, call your lender or credit card company to find out. Once you've got your debts listed with their interest rates, order them from the highest interest rate to the lowest interest rate. Using all of your savings except your emergency fund of three to six months of expenses, pay off your high interest debt first, then the next highest on the list, and the next, and so on until you're debt free.

I realize that you probably won't have adequate savings to pay all of your debts quickly. However, many people pile up money in a low-interest bank account while simultaneously running up debt in high-interest loans. If that has been you, the time for redemption has arrived. Use your savings to pay as much of your debt as possible, starting with the most expensive.

Michael and Susan have a home mortgage, three department store cards, two major credit cards, a car loan, and a home equity loan. They wrote their debts on a sheet of paper, listed the interest rates, and then ranked them on this list:

Michael and Susan's Debts	
Credit card	21.2%
Credit card	19.1%
Department store card	18.5%
Department store card	16%
Department store card	14.7%
Home equity loan	11%
Home mortgage	8%
Car loan	4.2%

Michael and Susan know that they should focus their extra money on their highest-interest credit card first, then the department store charges next, and so on down their list. Susan reminded Michael that they have amassed several thousand dollars in their bank savings account. Should they use that money to pay off some of their debts?

Yes, they decide. Even though it feels wrong to spend savings to pay off debt, it is usually the right move. The reason is simple. No savings account pays the high interest rates that credit cards charge. That means $100 in savings won't earn as much a return as a $100 balance on your credit card will cost. Michael and Susan would be earning, say, 3 percent on their savings while owing 21 percent interest on their debts.

Moving money from savings to pay off debt will jump-start your debt reduction plan. Be prudent about it, of course. Michael and Susan decided to use half their savings to pay off their credit cards while leaving enough for a six-month emergency reserve. That's a smart plan, one that you should copy.

I should note that not everybody agrees with this system of paying your most expensive debts first. There are other alternatives. My favorite is from Dave Ramsey, who suggests in his excellent book *Financial Peace* that you list your debts in descending order with the smallest balance first and the largest balance last. Start at the top of the list to pay off your smallest debt, then the next one, then the one bigger than that, and so on until all your debt is paid. This system pays no attention to interest rates. Instead, by paying off your smallest debts first, you see progress and are encouraged by the small successes to continue stalking your larger debt. Ramsey calls this technique the debt snowball.

I still prefer the system of paying expensive debt first because the numbers make more sense. However, the numbers are meaningless if you don't continue paying down the debt. Do whatever it takes to get your emotions behind your debt reduction plan. I don't care if you list your debts in order of the ugliest name to the prettiest. If that's what motivates you to keep paying them off, do it.

Consolidate into a Cheaper Loan

When you have exhausted your savings—and that might have been at the exact moment you made your debt list, because you have no savings—it's time to figure the best way to whittle your remaining debt to zero. Consolidating your many expensive debts into one inexpensive loan is a great strategy.

Look over Michael and Susan's debt list in the previous section. Notice that their home equity loan charges only 11 percent, while their credit cards charge higher rates. After paying part of their debt with their savings, could they move their remaining credit card debt into their home equity loan?

Absolutely. In fact, paying off high-interest debt is one of the most common uses of a home equity loan. After consolidating their credit card balances into their home equity loan, Michael and Susan are left with a debt list of only three items.

Michael and Susan's Debts After Consolidation	
Home equity loan	11%
Home mortgage	8%
Car loan	4.2%

The dollars they owe haven't changed a bit, but they have fewer bills to pay each month and their finance charges have dropped considerably. That's valuable progress.

Home equity loans aren't the only option for consolidating your debt. Banks offer plain consumer loans for whatever you want to buy. These days, they'll lend money to anybody for anything. Besides, your goal of consolidating high-interest debt in a low-interest loan makes good financial sense. The bank will see that you were making payments on the cards all along and should be able to make payments on the loan.

Now, you can run into problems with consolidating. If, for example, you consolidate your debts into one loan and extend that loan over five years, you might end up paying more interest than if you had just aggressively pursued paying the original loans in a shorter amount of time. The consolidation is a tool.

Consolidating by itself isn't your goal. Consolidate, then throw all of your might into. paying down the loan. Kill it, smash it, reduce it to zero, then invite your friends and family over to watch the note burn.

It will be a great day because you will have eliminated debt from your life.

When I graduated from college, I carried $2,780 of debt on credit cards that I used for buying books and food while I was a poor student. My first order of business was to get a good job at IBM. Within one week of starting work, I joined the company credit union and consolidated all of my credit card debt into a 12.5 percent loan. The minimum payment was $132 per month for two years. When all was said and done, I would have paid $377 in interest expenses.

That plan didn't sit well with me. I'd already been in debt for four years and was ready to get out immediately, not in another two years. So I tightened my belt and paid the loan off in three months. The total paid in interest expense was less than $50. The exhilaration of attacking the debt so aggressively kept me in high spirits during the three lean months. There was a reason for the sacrifice. I was fighting a war. There is no time for luxury during a war.

Wage War on Your Debt

Take a similar approach to your consolidations. Get all of the debt into one place, then attack with all your might. Don't feel satisfied that the consolidation has reduced your interest expense by several points. You're still in debt. Avoid relaxing and settling into a long payment schedule. Pay as much as you can each month. Chop the numbers down. Kill, kill, kill. Debt kills you, so you should kill debt. It's financial self-defense.

Do I seem like a madman? Maybe. But I'm a debt-free madman. See you in the asylum.

Staying Out of Debt in the Future

After you have escaped your existing debt, you will never acquire the bad kind of debt again. I mean that. Forget the flashy advertising. Forget the temptations. Forget the Joneses. Once you have experienced debt-free living, where every penny of yours is yours, you will never go into debt again.

That's what this little section is all about. You'll remember to spend less than you earn and learn to convert debt payments into savings.

Spend Less Than You Earn

You won't go into debt if you spend less than you earn. Before getting to this chapter, you examined your spending habits, found areas of waste, and came up with strategies for saving money. The money you freed up in the process went toward paying your debts. Now that you have escaped your debts, continue the strategies that made it possible. In fact, don't ever stop paying off your debt. Instead, you should . . .

Convert Debt Payments into Savings

Take the massive amounts of money you poured into your debt and redirect them into savings. If you paid $300 every month until your debt disappeared, congratulations! Now, point that $300 monthly payment into a savings account and start getting ahead. It will feel good to watch your money build the assets side of your net worth statement instead of the liabilities side.

If you paid an unusually large percentage of your income to the debt to pay it off quickly, you might want to save less than that. For instance, I lived on rice and water during the months that I paid off my credit card consolidation. I didn't want to continue living that way forever. Once the debt was paid, I began living a normal life again, but still managed to save several hundred dollars per month.

By building a solid foundation of savings and investments, you can "borrow" from yourself in the future. That's a great technique. Imagine that you wanted to buy a used car for $10,000. If

you have $20,000 sitting in mutual funds somewhere, lend your-
self the ten grand. Then, pay yourself back at a 10 percent rate of
interest.

Lending money to yourself is a great way to stay ahead of
debt. Plus, if the borrower ever defaults on your loan, you know
where to find the schmuck.

Using Credit Cards the Right Way

I have no objection to you destroying every one of your
credit cards. If you've read this far in the book and so abhor debt
that you will from now on buy everything with cash, then I've
accomplished a good thing in your life. The temptation of consumer debt is so powerful that avoiding it altogether is preferable
to the tiny benefit gained from using it the right way.

However, there is a way to use credit cards that benefits you,
not the lender. Used properly, credit cards offer you interest-free
loans every month. They are also convenient.

Never Use Department Store Cards

Get rid of all department store cards. They are unnecessary
and only serve to tempt you into buying the expensive merchandise at the card's store. Only expensive stores issue their
own credit cards. When was the last time you saw a 7-Eleven
charge card? Never, of course. The only stores that issue charge
cards are expensive department stores that fool you into carrying
an ad for the store that is also a financial noose with which to
hang yourself.

Take all of your department store cards and cut them up,
melt them, turn them into fishing lures, or mail them back to the
department store in an envelope marked "Your Death Traps
Enclosed."

Remember, any store large enough to issue its own charge
cards will also accept the major credit cards as well.

Keep No More Than Two Major Cards

Because you can get through life just fine with no credit cards, you can surely do fine with just one. No matter what your circumstances, however, there is never a need for more than two major credit cards.

With two cards, you can reserve one for personal use and one for business use. If you are an employee with no sideline businesses, then one card is plenty. Despite what the Visa and MasterCard ads tell you, they are both accepted just about anywhere. I know that each has managed to locate one store in lower Slobovia that does not accept the other's card, but for all realistic purposes both cards are equally effective around the world.

Find Cards with No Annual Fee

After you've determined to keep one or two credit cards, find ones with no annual fee. Because you will never carry a balance on your credit cards again, the annual interest rate is less important to you than the absence of a fee. It doesn't matter if you use a card with a 45 percent annual interest rate—as long as you pay your balance in full every month and are never charged.

You can get a list of no-fee and low-rate cards from Bankcard Holders of America, 524 Branch Drive, Salem, VA 24153, 703-389-5445. If you want still more information, try RAM Research *CardTrak*, PO Box 1700, Frederick, MD 21702, 301-695-4660, www.ramresearch.com. Bankcard Holders charges $4; RAM charges $5.

If your current cards come with no annual fee, then you don't have to do a thing.

Find Cards with Incentive Plans

To get really slick about your credit card purchases, consider using one that provides you with a kickback on all your purchases. Don't get distracted by incentives, though. That is, after all, why they're there. Card issuers hope to confuse stupid people with pictures of vacations and new cars.

Don't be stupid. By far, the most important part about credit cards is paying the balance every month. That part has nothing to do with the card you choose. The next most important part is choosing one with no annual fee.

Only after all of the basics are satisfied should you begin comparing incentive plans. Some cards offer free airline miles, others discounts on automobile purchases, others provide cash back, while still others give free gasoline. You get compensated as a percentage of what you charge on the card.

Naturally, being the informed person you are after reading this book, you would never let the incentive plan actually cause you to spend more on the card just to get more back. That would be stupid, because you will never get back anything worth more than what you spent to get it.

Don't choose an incentive plan based on the actual item you get in return. Always convert the bonuses into their cash value and then compare cards for the best one for you. You can always purchase the things they're giving away. Your goal is maximum cash value in your pocket for the spending you would do anyway.

For example, if one card offers 2 percent of all your purchases in the form of free gasoline, another offers 2 percent cash back, and another offers a frequent flier mile for every dollar you charge, here's how to choose.

The first two cards are a wash. They both give you 2 percent back. The value of the prize is still 2 percent of your purchases regardless of whether it comes as gasoline or greenbacks. The gasoline is just a gimmick—and a way to get you to buy that company's gasoline. The way to choose between those two cards is to look at the price of the company's gasoline. If it's competitive with other stations in your area, then the card is truly as valuable as the cash-back card. If the gasoline is more expensive than at other stations, then the cash-back card is a better deal. If the gasoline is cheaper than at other stations, the gasoline incentive card is a better deal.

Don't Use Airline Cards for Airlines You Can't Use!

As for the airline mileage card, begin by asking whether you would ever use the airline in question anyway. I know a friend who started a mileage credit card for an airline that doesn't even serve his area! There's somebody putting a lot of thought into his finances.

If the airline does serve your area and is one that you would use in the normal course of things, then the card is still a candidate.

Next, look at the airline's frequent flier plan. Does it take 15,000 miles for a free ticket, or 25,000, or 35,000? The more miles it takes, the less of a bargain it is to use the credit card. Do the miles expire? If so, you might be tempted to spend more just to get the necessary miles needed for a free ticket before you lose the miles you've already acquired. Look at the average price of the tickets to your typical destinations. Convert the value of the mileage plan into dollars, then compare it to the dollar value of the other two cards. Choose the best one.

What a mess, eh? Look at all the factors that can go into this relatively minor decision of which incentive plan to choose. I remind you again that confusion is the goal of the issuing companies. Everybody likes pretty pictures more than they like hard numbers. The card companies know that. They will try to keep you focused on the pictures of the incentive plan so you miss the fine print about annual fees and high interest rates.

These incentive plans are icing on the cake. Choose the most valuable one only after satisfying the most important card details first.

Pay Your Balance in Full for a Free Loan

To turn the tables on the evil credit card industry, all you need to do is pay the balance every month on your no-fee card. You will not be charged interest during the grace period. Thus, the joke is now on them. You get an interest-free loan every month with which to buy the items you would normally buy anyway.

There are cards out there that don't offer the so-called grace period, which is usually around twenty-five days. They are few and far between, but you should be aware of their insidious existence. Read the fine print on your credit card applications and never use a card with no grace period.

The best benefit of paying your balance every month is that you never acquire debt. But a close second is this interest-free grace period. Guess what? People with balances don't get the grace period anymore. As soon as you carry a balance from one month to the next, interest begins accruing on new purchases immediately. Not only do you build debt, you also lose the ability to use a credit card for free.

Right about here, I could go into all the details of how credit card interest is calculated. I could explain the average daily balance method as compared to the two-cycle method. But I won't. You know why? Because even explaining how interest is calculated might lead you to infer that if you get the right card, it's all right to carry a balance now and then.

It isn't. I'm explicitly telling you to avoid carrying a balance.

I'm sweating as I write. Please mumble that you understand by now. This issue is critical to your long-term success with money. You don't need to know how interest is calculated on credit cards because you will never be charged interest. You will pay your balance every month on time and enjoy the fruits of an interest-free grace period. Forever. There will be no exceptions.

Do you know why there will be no exceptions? Because the first time you ever miss a payment, you will have shown yourself that credit cards are too dangerous for you and you will cut all of them up immediately. You'll do it to send a message to the gazillionaire bankers rubbing their hands together for your money. You'll do it to get ahead in life.

A great way to guarantee that your balance is paid each month is to get a card from a credit union. Credit unions are special, not-for-profit financial institutions that you'll learn all about in chapter 5. They're similar to banks, but less greedy. Because they are not-for-profit, many credit unions will automatically transfer the full balance of your credit card from your checking account each month. You don't need to write a check or seal an envelope. There's no risk of being late and being charged interest. This, by the way, is the type of credit card I use. It's the best way to go.

Consider a Debit Card Instead

If you ever carry a balance and are forced to destroy all of your credit cards as instructed, do not despair. You can get all the convenience of credit cards with none of the risk by using a debit card.

A debit card works exactly like a credit card, except that instead of building a balance that must be paid each month, the money is taken directly from your checking account. You use debit cards like credit cards and ATM cards, but they work more like personal checks.

With the advent of debit cards, there is no longer the "convenience" excuse for carrying credit cards. A debit card is every bit as convenient. Most even have the Visa or MasterCard symbol right on them. Anywhere that Visa and MasterCard are accepted, so is your debit card.

"Wow!" you're thinking. "This is heaven on earth." Debit cards are pretty good news, but they're not without a few wrinkles. Some banks charge an annual fee, which you've come to see as a no-no. Some banks charge each time you use the card. That gets too expensive in a hurry. Other banks set limits on how much you can spend with the card.

This information should neither surprise nor scare you. You know by now that everybody is out to gouge you for your money. So of course some banks charge ridiculous fees.

The reason you don't need to be scared is because you are capable of reading the debit card application and calling the bank on the phone to clear up any issues that might be a problem. Being the smart manager of your own money, you know to look for a debit card that does not have an annual fee, does not charge each time you use the card, and does not set restrictive limits.

Most major banks, many investment companies, and quite a few credit unions offer debit cards. Check with your current institution for availability. If you end up shopping for a new financial institution, which is very likely after you read chapter 5, you can make the availability of a debit card one of your requirements.

Getting a Good Car Loan and a Cheap Price

As much as I harped in chapter 2 about the evils of financing a new automobile, I realize that you might do it anyway. If you're going to get a new car with a shiny new loan attached, at least minimize the damage by getting a good deal on the loan and a low price on the car. This section explains how.

Please notice that this discussion takes place in a chapter about the bad kind of debt. Even though I'm about to explain the way to get a good deal on your new car, a car loan is still the bad kind of debt. You are borrowing money for something that depreciates quicker than it drives. I strongly discourage buying new cars, for all the reasons you read about in chapter 2. In fact, before continuing through this section, perhaps you'd like to reread my thoughts on the merits of used automobiles. If so, turn back to page 22.

All right, so you've been forewarned and you still want to buy a new car. Let's try to keep the financial carnage to a minimum.

Conduct Thorough Research

Decide exactly why you're buying a car. If it's to get the kids around, then you won't need to research two-seat sports cars. If it's to impress the folks at the office, then you can safely ignore station wagons and minivans. If it's to maximize your fuel efficiency around town, sport utility vehicles are out of the question.

Once you have a ballpark idea for the type of car you want, start reading about that category. Pick up magazines, buy or borrow *Consumer Reports Annual Auto Issue*, and conduct research on the Internet. Be sure to check on the insurance and maintenance costs of cars you're considering. Also, talk to your friends and family. Remember the discussion about keeping the "personal" in personal finance? Here's where it can pay off.

The Basic Purpose of Cars Hasn't Changed in Fifty Years

Find cars that have high customer satisfaction ratings. Look for cars that have won awards. Write on your list of prospective new cars the ones that rate high in the areas that are important to you. Do you want good fuel economy? Do you want a lot of trunk space? Is acceleration important to you? Only you know the answers to those questions, and only you can find the makes and models that fit the kind of car you want to buy.

When you've narrowed your list of prospective cars from a general category to a handful of possibilities, make a list of the features that you want. Armed with this later, you will be able to resist add-ons that you'd never thought of. If you didn't think of them ahead of time, you probably don't need them. I mean, really, how much have automobile basics changed in the past fifty years? Not much. No matter how nifty they look, cars are still just a way to drive from here to there. Whatever the latest trendy item is—inertial navigation, talking weather monitors, seat heaters, and so on—you'll be fine without.

So write down whether you want air-conditioning, automatic or standard transmission, power windows and locks, deluxe stereo, sunroof, multiple driver settings, and so on down the list. Look it over carefully, discuss it with your family, talk to your friends again. Finalize the list until your dream car has all the ingredients that will make this whopper of a purchase worthwhile.

Thus armed, you are ready for a first test drive. You are not buying at this point. Hammer that into your head. You will not tell the dealer how much you're willing to pay, when you plan to buy, why your life is incomplete without this particular car, and so on. None of their tricks will work on you because you are only test driving. Say it every five minutes on your way from dealer to dealer. Then, when you step from the car and are immediately greeted by a sales person, the first thing you are to blurt is, "I am here for a test drive only. I am not buying today. Quit smiling at me and get the keys to that car over there."

If you still like the car after the test drive and after seeing the sticker price, gather all the information the dealership has to offer. Take the brochures, pens, miniature models, and crib sheets home with you.

When you've test driven and gathered information on each car, carefully read all of it and further consider which is best. Create an exact profile of that car. Write down its make, model, color, transmission, and so on. You know from your trip to the dealerships approximately how much they're asking. That will be helpful in the next section.

Start at a Bank or Credit Union

You want to be completely prepared to buy when you return to the car dealership the second time around. Call several banks and your credit union, if you have one, to see who is offering the best rates on car loans. Go to that financial institution. The rates at the credit union will usually be better. But if not, or if you aren't a member of a credit union, go to the bank with the best rate.

Ask to be preapproved for the automobile loan. Preapproval means that the bank has inspected your financial qualifications and has determined ahead of time that you are approved for a loan up to a certain amount, say $20,000. With that piece of paper, you are effectively walking into the dealership with a blank check that you can write in any amount up to twenty grand.

Be sure to negotiate with the bank loan officer. If you can get another half-point or full point of interest taken off the loan, it's worth a little haggling. If not, it was worth a shot. One thing is certain. If you don't ask, the rate won't get any lower than what was first offered.

Pay a Lot and Pay the Rest Quickly

Ideally, you would be able to "borrow" the money from yourself and pay the car dealer with cash. The feistier among you might try the old argument that it makes sense to get a bank loan if you can invest the money that you would have used to pay cash. Making 10 percent in the stock market while paying a 5 percent loan will put you ahead.

Sure it will, but there's more to the story. Ask yourself where you intend to get the money to make loan payments. If you plan to get it from the invested money that would have been used in place of the car loan, then the amount will dwindle over time and it usually will not earn enough to keep pace with the interest expense of the loan. If you plan to get the payments from your income, then you're still using cash that could have been invested elsewhere. In almost all cases, paying cash is cheaper than borrowing money.

Because few people are able to pay today's new-car sticker

prices with cash, the next best thing is to get as close to paying cash as possible. That means making as large a down payment as you can. Be careful when deciding whether to pay cash or how much to put as a down payment. If it means obliterating all of your savings, including your three- to six-month emergency fund, then don't do it. Go for a smaller down payment. Your emergency fund is critical to feeling secure.

Once you've put as much down as you can afford, keep the remaining payment plan as short as possible. This takes discipline because longer loans result in lower monthly payments and might even allow you to purchase a more expensive car. Oh swell, just what you need. Don't think in monthly increments. You've risen above that now and are a person who soaks up the entire picture of your life, not whether you can scramble through one month at a time.

Longer loans mean more interest paid to the lender. In addition, you will usually be charged a higher rate of interest. It's a double whammy. Keep the loan as short as possible, preferably two years or less.

Never take a loan for a term longer than you expect to drive the car. If you have a five-year loan and drive your car for only three years, the car's resale value will not be enough to pay the loan in full. You'll have payments even after you sell your car. Then, if you buy another new car to replace the one you just sold, you'll have another loan on top of the one you are paying for the old car that you don't even own anymore.

That is not a neat way to manage your money. If you make a financial blunder that big, your friends and family will forever wonder why you even bothered to read this book.

So, put as much cash into the deal as you can afford without destroying your financial base, then pay the rest of the loan off as quickly as possible.

Do Not Lease

Leasing has become popular because it allows you to put no money down and make low monthly payments on cars that you could otherwise never afford to drive. Well, guess what? If you can't afford to buy the car, you should own a cheaper one instead of renting the more expensive one.

That's all it amounts to. They don't call it renting because then you would understand that you will never own the automobile. If they call it leasing, it sounds more official and you might just be suckered into doing it.

Don't be. Leasing is a cheaper way to have an automobile if you would otherwise buy a new one every two years. See the danger in it? When you adopt a leasing mentality, you are encouraged to change cars every couple years. You will never own one. You will make car payments forever. Car makers and dealers love leasing because it brings ignorant customers back to pay more money every twenty-four months.

It's no coincidence that leases are difficult for most people to understand. Dealers and leasing companies don't want you to understand anything except the lure of no money down and low monthly payments. For instance, if you ask what interest rate you will be charged, the dealer might say, "There's no interest rate. There's only the lease rate."

Since you have no idea that the lease rate and interest rate are the exact same thing, you might not know to press further and again ask for the percentage. If you do press further, you might be told that "there is no percentage figure. The leasing company uses a simple money factor to compute your payment."

Hmm, there's another term you've never heard. Now you're feeling like a moron and the dealer is acting impatient. Come on, quit asking so many pesky questions. Just sign on the line and drive your new car home.

But you decide to ask for the money factor even though you haven't the foggiest idea what a money factor is. So he tells you that the money factor for your particular lease happens to be 0.0054.

That figure is utterly meaningless to you by itself, but I'll tell you how to turn it into the annual interest rate. Simply multiply by twenty-four. So in this case, your lease comes with a 13 percent interest rate.

Avoid the Shiny New Lease

"Oh, and one last thing," the salesman says. "You can only drive the leased car twelve thousand miles per year. Additional driving will cost you twenty-five cents per mile." These figures differ from lease to lease, but the ones you just read are common.

See why leasing is a drag? You'll navigate uncharted waters filled with sharks who want to squeeze every penny out of your budget. All this hassle for the privilege of renting your cars forever and only driving them a specified number of miles per year. Where's the freedom of the open road? Where's the pride of ownership? Where's anything that makes sense?

Leasing capitalizes on the human desire to impress. You don't want just any car, you want the fastest and shiniest so that everybody knows how successful you are. Forget that. Who are you really trying to impress? Most people will either not notice what you drive or they will be jealous of your having a better car than they do. You will be spending a boatload of money to be ignored or hated.

Don't spend money to impress people. Spend money to get what you need from life. A perpetual rental car ain't what you need. Do not lease.

Out-deal the Dealer

In their book *You Have More Than You Think*, David and Tom Gardner suggest an excellent way to deal with car dealers. Use your fax machine. That's right. You've already specified on your list what you want in a new car. Put it in a letter and fax it to the dealers in your area. Include only your fax number on the cover sheet. That way they won't be able to call and bother you.

Here's an example of how your letter might read:

Dear Sir or Madam:
  I am buying a new car soon. On this fax, I have listed the model of the car and the features that I want included. I am taking bids from local dealers. I will look over the bids and choose which car to purchase.
  When you bid, please include all costs, itemized by option; all dealership fees; and all taxes due. Fax your bid to me at the number on the cover sheet.

By faxing your request, you avoid all the pressure of the lot. The dealers will fax back their best bids and you can then look them over and decide which one to patronize. You may be surprised at how far apart many of the bids are. It's not uncommon to save thousands of dollars with this one simple step.

If you enjoyed the process and would like to squeeze it for all it's worth, send a second fax to dealerships farther away than those receiving the first fax. Use the same letter, but this time include the lowest bid you received from the first round of bidding. You'll see if anybody farther from your home can beat the lowest nearby bidder by enough to make the drive worthwhile.

When you've faxed and collected bids to your heart's content, focus on your two best bidders. Call the one in second place, and make an offer below the price of your best bidder. If the second-place bidder bites, take it. If not, go with the lowest offer. I think the Gardner fax plan is an excellent system to keep you out of harm's way.

Buy at the Right Time

When you have your best bids and are ready to buy, wait for the right time. Unfortunately, the right time is different depending on who you ask.

Some former car salesmen who have revealed all in their books and videos, say that the dead of winter is the best time to buy a new car because nobody else is out looking. The sales force is sitting behind windows, watching the rain drizzle or the snow fall, knowing that they might not earn enough to pay the rent. Because they're eager for business, you can swoop in and get a good deal.

Other experts in this field say that fall is the best time to buy a new car because the new models for the next year are just being released. The prices on current year models will soften up because dealers are eager to move them off the lot to make room for the newer, more expensive models.

It looks like you can take your pick of seasons. But one thing that almost everybody agrees on is that buying at the end of the month is best.

The reason is simple. Dealers work on monthly quotas. They are given quotas from auto manufacturers, and they pass those quotas down to their sales force. In the beginning of the month, sales people are relaxed and eager to haggle for high prices. They're under no pressure. If they don't make a sale today, there's always tomorrow. If not tomorrow, then next week. There's a whole month to go.

But at the end of the month, there are fewer tomorrows. The pressure is on and it's time to make sales at lower prices if necessary. That's when you should appear, able to help the dealer make his quota if you get your cheap price. You give a little, you get a little back.

You can experiment with the seasonal bit all you want. I'm not sure that it matters much. But I am confident that you will be giving yourself a leg up by buying your car during the last week of the month.

Consider Dealer Financing

Even though you will be armed with a preapproved loan from a bank or credit union, take a quick look at what the dealer is offering. Occasionally, special promotions will allow you to finance your car at interest rates as low as one or two percent. Because the whole point of the incredibly low-interest financing is to get you to buy a car on the spot, it's easy to apply for and get dealer financing on the same day you went to buy the car with your preapproved loan.

As always, be on your guard. Be careful of special conditions attached to the loan, such as no money down and a seventy-two-month duration and a gradually increasing interest rate. They'll try whatever it takes to get your money. Be especially cautious of the "no money down" bit. Any time you hear that, you should immediately translate to "lots of interest expense instead."

Look at what the dealer financing has to offer, compare it with your preapproved loan from your credit union or bank, and choose the best one.

Another point: Sometimes you can get a half to one point knocked off your interest rate if the dealer is competing against a preapproved loan from a bank.

No Silly, Expensive Options

Options are the most profitable part of the car. Hence, dealers will work hard to sell you as many as they can. Some might be important to you, and you'll know by looking over the list you made ahead of time. Others are plain silly and expensive.

Take fabric protection, paint sealant, and rustproofing. Altogether, they can add more than $1,000 to the price of your car. That's a lot to pay for completely unnecessary procedures.

Fabrics used in cars these days are already resistant to spills and wear. No spray-on coating is going to do much more for the long-term. If you're really worried about the interior of your car, buy some cheap seat covers.

Even They Can Do Without Rustproofing

As for paint sealant and rustproofing, give me a break. When was the last time you heard of a new car rusting? We're not talking about a garden tool that sits in the dirt and gets rained on. We're talking about your car. Are you planning to park it in a swamp? Probably not. Have you noticed that rainwater beads up and runs off your car naturally? Of course you have. It also works at the car wash. It's like magic, and it happens without any special sealant or rustproofer.

Of all the options dealers will try to push on you, none is more costly and useless than the extended warranty. The repairs that it covers are so catastrophic that it will pay only a small part of the total expense. Extended warranty deductibles are so high that they are never used for the small things that usually go wrong. What more is there to say? An extended warranty doesn't pay for the big things or the little things. Great deal. Besides, the standard warranty on most new cars is pretty comprehensive.

Enjoy Your New Car

By following this methodical approach to buying a new car, you will avoid common mistakes and get a good deal you can be proud of.

You have educated yourself in the type of car you want, so you won't be unduly influenced by special promotions or nifty displays or any of the other chicanery that goes on at the dealership. You have secured a good interest rate on a preapproved loan and compared it to dealer financing. You have successfully negotiated a good price without ever staring into the mesmerizing eyes of a car sales rep. You understand why you don't need silly, expensive options.

Very impressive. Enjoy your new car!

Getting a Good Home Equity Loan

Notice that, like the previous section on car loans, this discussion takes place in the chapter about the bad kind of debt. That's not a mistake. Home equity loans, or HELs, haven't always been called that. They used to be called second mortgages because that's what they are. Marketing departments realized that by calling them home equity loans or home equity lines of credit, you might be fooled into thinking they were sound investments, just like buying your home might have been.

Well, they're not investments. They're mortgage loans for property you've already invested in and, more specifically, the portion of the property that you've already paid for. You borrow against the value of your home minus the money you still owe on the mortgage.

For instance, if you bought your home for $250,000 and you still owe $100,000 on your mortgage, you have $150,000 in equity against which you can borrow. Notice that as the value of your home appreciates, your equity rises. If the home you paid $250,000 for is now worth $350,000 and you owe the same $100,000 on your mortgage, you have $250,000 in equity.

Most financial institutions will lend you up to 80 percent of your equity. In the previous example, you could borrow up to 80 percent of the $250,000—that's a cool $200,000. HELs work a lot like credit cards, except that the bank takes your home when you don't pay.

There are two advantages to using a home equity loan. First, it will charge a lower interest rate than your credit cards and many other types of loans. Second, the interest you pay will be tax deductible. For these two reasons, HELs can be a smart way to consolidate higher-interest debt into one place. Then, you can focus all of your debt payment on the one loan instead of paying off six different credit cards and three other loans.

I remind you from the loan consolidation section on page 51 that you need to pay off your home equity loan as quickly as possible. Many people use HELs to get temporary relief from a barrage of loan payments. They consolidate everything into the HEL, and then take their sweet time repaying. Most HELs allow you to set your own monthly payment.

Too many eyes light up at that capability. You need to resist the temptation to pay $20 for the next sixty years. With that approach, you would have been better off keeping your debt in the high-interest loans with faster repayment schedules.

If you do use an HEL to consolidate your expensive debts, pay it off at least as quickly as you were paying the initial debts. To get ahead of the game, pay as much as you can possibly afford. Get that debt to zero.

Hopefully you are making a determined effort to escape all of your debt and have chosen an HEL as the way to do it. In that case, great. I'm behind you 100 percent. Here are a couple items to watch for when you shop for the loan.

Beware the Upfront Fees

Lenders charge fees for all sorts of itemized costs before granting you a home equity loan. These can range from a few hundred to several thousand dollars. As with car loans, you should always shop around for the best bargain.

Add the fees to the rest of the loan and make sure that it's still the smart choice. If you owe $4,000 on credit cards that you intend to pay off within one year, then a $4,500 HEL paid in the same amount of time isn't smart. Even with the high interest expense on the credit cards, you won't exceed the additional $500 tacked onto the HEL. Your aggressive monthly payments will quickly reduce the $4,000 owed on the cards. There will be less money borrowed at the high interest rate as each month goes by and you pay off the debt. Therefore, the amount you'd pay in interest on the credit cards during your "payoff" year would not add up to the $500 that the HEL would cost.

Of course, sometimes the HEL does make sense. Look at the fees, compare the interest savings, and choose wisely.

Choose the Right Rate

Naturally, you want as low an interest rate as possible on your HEL. You usually have the choice between a variable rate and a fixed rate.

Variable rates will usually be lower than fixed rates at the outset. But, because they're variable, they can rise over time. Ask the loan officer how high your payments could go during your aggressive payoff schedule.

If the variable rate could rise enough to extend your payoff schedule, you should consider a fixed rate that will allow you to pay off the loan on time. If the variable seems to work within your aggressive time frame and you can save a few percentage points, then choose it.

Checking Your Credit Report

Your borrowing history is tracked by credit agencies and contained in something called your credit report. The report shows your birth date, Social Security number, job history, current and previous addresses, and the name of your spouse. Then it displays every one of your credit relationships, like credit cards and loans.

When you apply for a loan or an apartment or just about anything that will involve your making regular payments, the person deciding whether to accept your application will usually check your credit report. They'll see how long you've had each account, how much you owe, whether you've consistently paid on time, and how deeply you could go into hock on your available credit.

Because your credit report is such a central part of the lending process, it's a good idea to know how it looks. You can order your own credit report at any time from credit agencies. Two of the biggest are Experian (formerly TRW) and Equifax.

To obtain your credit report, send a check for $9 to Experian National Consumer Assistance Center, P.O. Box 2104, Allen, TX 75013-2104; or, to Equifax Information Service Center, P.O. Box 740241, Atlanta, GA 30374-0241. You can also order your credit report by calling Experian at 888-397-3742 or Equifax at 800-685-1111. Include your full name, maiden name, current address, addresses for the past five years, Social Security number, telephone number, and date of birth. If you are denied credit or turned down for a loan, all the credit agencies are legally required to send you a free report if you ask within thirty days.

When the report arrives, look it over carefully for any mistakes. Credit bureaus are notorious for getting the information wrong. Something like a misspelled name is no big deal, but accidentally telling the world that you've defaulted on your mortgage payment could cause problems.

If you find mistakes, immediately mail a letter to the credit agency or agencies. They will investigate and get back to you. If they agree that they made a mistake, you should ask that they resend the report to all who received the incorrect one. The agencies will do so free of charge.

If the agencies disagree with your finding, you can have them attach your explanation to the credit report for those who request it in the future.

You can take a tiny bit of comfort in the fact that most bad credit information disappears from your report after seven years. Even bankruptcies go away in ten years. If you were hoping for a car loan, however, this is small comfort indeed.

Bankruptcy as a Fresh Start

Oh boy. I can see my grandfather and father biting their knuckles at the mere mention of that "B" word. Bankruptcy is definitely the last resort. It tells the financial community that you are unable to pay your debts and blacklists you for ten years. You'll be one of the highest lending risks on two feet.

There are two types of bankruptcy. Chapter 7 absolves you of certain debts, such as credit card balances, medical bills, rent, utilities, and car loans. It's the most sensible form of bankruptcy for people who carry a lot of the debt that can be canceled.

Chapter 13 does not get rid of any debt. Instead, it plans out a payment schedule over several years and keeps your creditors at a distance. But it doesn't eliminate anything. For most people, Chapter 7 is the way to go. If you're going to be blacklisted anyway, you might as well be blacklisted with no debt.

For Certain Debts, This May Be Your Only Means of Escape

There are certain debts that are not escapable through bankruptcy. They include taxes, student loans, child support, and alimony. At best, the courts can work out a reasonable schedule of payment under Chapter 13, but aside from leaving the country in a straw hat and dark glasses, you can't get away from certain debts.

Before you decide that bankruptcy is your only option, contact the Consumer Credit Counseling Service at 800-388-2227. CCCS will help you figure out better options for beating your debt. They will even contact lenders to negotiate better rates and payment schedules. The basic fee charged by CCCS is $9 per month, but the fee is waived if you cannot afford it.

There is something you should know about CCCS. It's a nonprofit educational service to help people pay their debts, but it is funded by credit card issuers. That's not exactly an unbiased sponsorship base. CCCS counselors will hardly ever recommend bankruptcy, even if it appears to be the only option.

If you've tried reworking your payment schedules, lowering your interest rates, and cutting expenses, and you still can't escape your debt, then it's time to look at bankruptcy. Pick up a copy of *How to File for Bankruptcy* published by Nolo Press. It contains all the instructions and forms you will need.

You simply fill out the forms and submit them with a fee of around $200 to a federal bankruptcy court. Immediately, creditors must stop pursuing you. They wait for a judge's decision on the matter. If the judge allows your case to proceed, it's likely that many of your qualifying debts will be erased. It is also likely that you will lose some of your assets to help compensate your creditors.

Contrary to popular belief, you won't walk out of bankruptcy court in a barrel and suspenders. You are usually allowed to keep your home, car, basic furnishings, clothing, and retirement accounts.

Surprisingly, you won't even be denied credit for very long. Many people who declare bankruptcy are carrying brand new credit cards within a couple years. That's how unbelievably available credit has become.

Doesn't sound so bad, does it? Heck, let's all go in together and drive banks out of business. We'll have a ball charging up hundreds of thousands of dollars in consumable items that can't be seized when we go belly up. Yeah, Citicorp and Chase Manhattan and Bank of America and all you other fat-cat card companies. We're all getting platinum cards and we're going out on the town big time every night for months on end. We're renting limousines and eating lobster and getting manicures and massages. Nothing you can seize. We'll laugh at your collection notices and once we're content on all that good food and relaxed from our massages, we'll roll into bankruptcy court and thumb our noses at you.

Of course, I'm joking. I hate the marketing of credit so much that I wouldn't be too upset to see that incident happen. But we're not all in it together, and you would be part of a few people declaring bankruptcy.

There are serious drawbacks to declaring bankruptcy. First, it destroys your credit for ten years. While that may not prevent you from getting a high-rate credit card—something that is truly baffling to me—it can prevent you from getting important items like a job. Many employers will look at your credit history. If they see *bankruptcy* in big black letters, that tells them that you are not responsible with your money. It may lead them to think that you will not be responsible with company money either.

Remember that you will lose much of your property. It's beyond your control. You throw your finances across a table and the court decides who gets what. It may not be you, and you could end up miserable with what you have left.

If you have any cosigners on loans, you are throwing the entire burden of your debts on them. Because cosigners are often family and friends, you will place a grave strain on your most important relationships.

Also, the cute scenario I described above about all of us eating lobster for six months and then declaring bankruptcy would not work. Bankruptcies can be challenged for suspected fraud, and that one would be. Other behavior that usually leads to a bankruptcy challenge includes getting large cash advances, attempting to hide property, and transferring property ownership from you to another family member. Anything along these lines looks like you were planning bankruptcy all along. Your creditors will challenge your filing and probably succeed in getting it thrown out of court.

Perhaps most important of all, it's pretty unpleasant to declare bankruptcy. It's hard not to feel some sense of failure when you borrow money from somebody and then refuse to pay it back.

Knowing everything you know about the pros and cons of bankruptcy, give careful thought to whether it's the right choice for you. If so, at least treat it as a fresh start, not a clear balance to begin acquiring debt again.

After your bankruptcy, be financially responsible. Don't immediately start looking for companies that will issue you a high-risk credit card. Accepting the credit card is the highest risk of all.

Purchase everything with cash. That way you can slowly reconstruct a life for yourself based on strong financial principles. You will never go into debt again.

Now *that's* a fresh start.

4 / Managing the Good Kind of Debt

Having firmly established my general disdain of debt in chapter 3, I feel comfortable revealing to you now that not all debt is bad.

In investment terminology, the good kind of debt is called leverage. Leverage occurs when you use somebody else's money to acquire enough wealth to pay them back with interest and still have profit left for yourself. In this chapter, you'll learn common ways to use leverage to get ahead.

When Debt Works in Your Favor

As you know from your reading in chapter 3, bad debt is money borrowed to buy something that decreases in value. A new car costing $20,000 financed at 8 percent over three years will cost you $22,562. When the loan is paid off, the car that you own will be worth around $12,000. Paying $22,562 for a $12,000 car is not financially sound. Doing it repeatedly with every car you drive leads to a lifetime of wasted money. Doing it at the same time on credit cards and home equity loans and consumer debt can sink any household budget in a hurry.

Good debt, on the other hand, borrows $12,000 to pay for something that is worth $22,562 when you finally own it. Doing it repeatedly leads to a lifetime of amassing wealth with other people's money. The good kind of debt is good for everybody. The lender makes money because you pay interest on the amount that you borrowed. You make money because you end up owning something worth more than the amount you borrowed. The seller makes money because you bought the item for sale.

As I mentioned in the chapter introduction, the good kind of debt is known in the investment world as leverage. Sophisticated investors use leverage all the time. They borrow money from a broker or bank and use it to purchase stocks that they think will rise in value, far surpassing the amount of interest due on the loan. At a certain point, they sell the stock at a profit, pay back the loan in full, and pocket the remaining profit. Notice that the investor didn't use a dime of his own money. Using nothing but borrowed money, he was able to turn a profit in the stock market.

Of course, there is a down side. What if he had borrowed the money, bought the stock, and the price had dropped instead of risen? Then he might have to sell the stock at a loss and dip into his own money to pay back the lender with interest.

Most people will never use the good kind of debt as leverage in the stock market. Instead, they will use it to buy homes, go to college, and build a business.

Home Loans

Remember that you should spend no more than 28 percent of your monthly take-home pay on housing. I don't want you to get too excited about borrowing money for a home and then buy the biggest mansion in town. Even though you're able to buy more house than you can actually afford, you don't want to buy *too* much more. If you do, you might not be living in it for long.

Here's how leverage works with home buying. Let's say you bought a home for $250,000. You put 20 percent down and borrowed the remainder. That's $50,000 of your cash and a $200,000 mortgage.

A year later, you sell that house for $350,000. At first glance, it looks like you made a quick 40 percent profit. That's $100,000 made on a $250,000 purchase. Making a 40 percent profit in one year is just dandy. However, you actually did even better. You invested only $50,000 of your money in the home. Therefore, you made a quick 100 percent profit. That's $100,000 made on your $50,000 investment. You profited not only on your down payment, but on the borrowed mortgage as well.

In addition to all this cause for champagne popping, you had a fine home to live in for a year. The benefits of owning your home go way beyond number crunching. It's emotionally satisfying. It's the American dream and, I've noticed, the dream of quite a few other nationalities.

Now the bad news. A home owner can lose money on a home. Instead of selling the $250,000 home for $350,000, what if you could get only $200,000? Suddenly, you have only enough money to pay the bank its mortgage. You lost 100 percent of your down payment and will need to scrounge around for the interest due.

The bad news is not enough reason to shy away from buying a home. Most do appreciate in value. Besides, don't forget that a home is a place to live. If it is worth less on paper than you paid for it, why does that matter to you if you don't intend to sell? It doesn't. You can still mow the lawn, refinish the den, and put up holiday decorations every year.

Whether to Buy or Rent

As great as buying a home seems, there are times when renting makes sense. Don't automatically assume that people who rent are financially ignorant or have not risen to their station in life. If you are currently renting, do not feel an undue amount of pressure to run out and buy a home.

Take a careful look at several factors to help you decide whether to buy or rent. Those factors are the cost of owning, how long you will live in the area, and the opportunity cost of buying.

The Cost of Owning

The first consideration is whether you can afford the monthly payment. Keeping it below 28 percent of your monthly take-home pay might make it impossible for you to purchase a home right now. People in expensive cities face that problem all the time.

A $300,000 mortgage for thirty years at 7 percent will cost around $2,000 per month. That means you would need to bring home $7,000 per month to keep your housing payment within the healthy 28 percent range. Few people bring home $7,000 per month.

Does that mean that every homeowner in an expensive city makes gobs of money? No. It means that to maintain a healthy financial situation, they need to cut back in other areas. They will probably be paying more than 28 percent of their monthly take-home on housing. To compensate, they could dine out less, take public transportation, and avoid all credit card debt. Dining at home, incidentally, should be a pleasure. Why would you bother buying the home if you didn't intend to hang out there?

Let's run through a few numbers to help you decide if you can afford a home in your area. When you take out a mortgage from a lender, your home is used to secure the loan. That means that if you default, the lender can take your home away from you. Your monthly payments consist of principal and interest. The amount you borrow is the principal, the rest of the expense of the mortgage is the interest. Because the duration of most mortgages is so long, the interest paid is usually far more than the principal. Amazing but true. A $100,000 mortgage borrowed for thirty years at 10 percent costs you the $100,000 principal plus $215,925 in interest.

Below is a chart from Fannie Mae, a private company chartered by Congress to provide lenders with money to lend for home mortgages. Fannie's real name is Federal National Mortgage Association, but most people prefer Fannie Mae.

The chart shows the monthly payment on a mortgage of $1,000. To get the amount you would owe on a more expensive loan, just multiply the payment by the number of thousands you are borrowing. For instance, if you are borrowing $300,000 for thirty years at 7 percent, you would multiply the chart factor of 6.66 by 300. That gives you a monthly payment of $1,998.

Monthly Loan Payment Table Equal Monthly Payments To Amortize $1,000			
Interest Rate	15 Years	20 Years	30 Years
5.0%	$7.91	$6.60	$5.37
5.5%	8.18	6.88	5.68
6.0%	8.44	7.17	6.00
6.5%	8.72	7.46	6.33
7.0%	8.99	7.76	6.66
7.5%	9.28	8.06	7.00
8.0%	9.56	8.37	7.34
8.5%	9.85	8.69	7.69
9.0%	10.15	9.00	8.05
9.5%	10.45	9.33	8.41
10.0%	10.75	9.66	8.78
10.5%	11.06	9.99	9.15

The interest paid on a home mortgage is deductible from your income for tax purposes. That's a nice little break, and important enough to factor into the home buying decision. On the worksheet you're about to fill in, you will need to know your federal income tax rate. Here are the tax brackets for 1998:

1998 Federal Income Tax Brackets and Rates		
Singles Taxable Income	Married Filing Jointly Taxable Income	Federal Income Tax Rate
$0 to $25,350	$0 to $42,350	15%
25,350 to 61,400	42,350 to 102,300	28%
61,400 to 128,100	102,300 to 155,950	31%
128,100 to 278,450	155,950 to 278,450	36%
278,450 and up	278,450 and up	39.6%

In addition to the principal and interest you pay on the loan, you also need to pay property tax. For a precise figure in your

area, call a real estate agent or mortgage lender. If you can't find
your local rate, use the national average of 1.5 percent of your
property's value. Divide by 12 to get the amount you'll pay each
month in taxes. For instance, a person who lives in a $250,000
home at a 1.5 percent property tax rate pays $3,750 every year.
That's $312 every month on top of the mortgage payment.

All right, you now have everything you need to fill in the
cost of home ownership worksheet, which is next. I will use our
old friends Michael and Susan as an example to help you see how
the worksheet calculates the numbers. The worksheet assumes a
fixed-rate mortgage.

Monthly Cost of Owning a Home		
Item	Michael and Susan	You
1. Write your monthly mortgage payment	$760	$
2. Add monthly property taxes	$180	+ $
3. To get the total of your mortgage and property taxes	$940	= $
4. Write your income tax rate	28%	%
5. Multiply line 3 by line 4 to get your tax benefit	$263	= $
6. Subtract line 5 from line 3 to get the after-tax cost of your mortgage and taxes	$677	$
7. Add your monthly maintenance costs (1.5% of your home value, divided by 12 months in the year)	$180	+ $
8. And your monthly insurance costs ($50 to $100 based on home value)	$75	+ $
9. To get the total monthly cost of owning your home	$932	= $

Look at line 9 from your worksheet. If it is less than the
monthly rent you are paying now, buying is the right choice for
you. If not, you'll need to decide whether the extra expense is
worth the personal satisfaction of owning.

Michael and Susan were surprised to find that they are paying less to own their home than it would cost for them to rent a comparable home in their area.

How Long You Will Live in the Area

In addition to the price itself, the process of buying a home is expensive. There are points and fees on the mortgage, inspection charges, agent commissions, title insurance, and moving costs. All of that adds up to a pretty penny.

In most cases, you will not recoup these basic costs until the value of your home has risen about 15 percent. Unless you're in a very hot market at the right time, it will take at least a few years for your home to appreciate 15 percent.

That means that you should not buy a home unless you intend to live in it for at least three years, preferably longer. That's why so many young workers at their first jobs do not buy homes immediately. It's common to jump from one job to another early in a career. Moving from San Francisco to Seattle to Boston to Miami to Denver is easy when it just means ending one rental agreement and starting another. It's hard when it means selling one home and buying another.

Finally, the longer you own a home, the cheaper its payment will become when compared to renting. As inflation steadily rises, so do rents. Of course, property taxes and insurance may also rise but they will hopefully be more than offset by the rising value of the home. With a fixed-rate mortgage, the basic house payment will stay constant.

To illustrate, look at this table comparing the cost of owning a $200,000 home with renting it for $1,000 per month. The table assumes a mortgage of $160,000 financed at a fixed rate of 7 percent for thirty years. Also, it assumes that inflation will cook along at 3 percent per year, gradually driving higher the cost of insurance, property taxes, upkeep, and rental prices.

Thirty Years of Owning versus Renting		
Year	Monthly Ownership	Monthly Rent
1	$1,187	$1,000
5	$1,239	$1,125
10	$1,313	$1,300
15	$1,401	$1,500
30	$1,755	$2,360

Looking at the table, you can see that even if today it is slightly more expensive to own a home than to rent one, owning might still be the better choice if you are going to stay awhile. Not only will you build equity in a property that is increasing in value, you will eventually be paying less each month than if you rented a comparable property.

In expensive parts of the country, this benefit doesn't usually exist. In San Francisco, New York, and Los Angeles, it is almost always cheaper to rent than to buy. Nonetheless, the appreciation of home values can offset the higher monthly payments even in such expensive areas.

The Opportunity Cost of Buying

There are times when you make more money by investing outside the cost of a home. That is the situation that faced me when I moved to Los Angeles a few years back. I had enough money to buy a home, but was making a lot in the raging stock market. I believed that I could continue making more money in stocks than I could in the LA housing market. Because homes in LA are expensive, buying one would have taken a large percentage of my money from the stock market, thus making the opportunity cost of a home very high.

If I had moved to a small town in the Midwest, I could have found a comfortable home for less than $30,000. At that bargain price, I would have purchased it without a moment's thought. I would have owned my home and still had plenty of money to invest in the stock market.

Now, a word of caution. Unless you know what you're doing

Even When the Market Falls, You Can Still Live in Your Home

in the stock market, you probably should not pit your stock-picking skills against the appreciation of the real estate market. When you lose money in the stock market, it's gone. When you lose money in your home, it's worth less on paper but you can still live in it. You can't live in a cheap stock. That comparison is oversimplified, but will suffice for now.

If you have a sizable investment portfolio from which you would draw to make the down payment on a home, consider whether you think the home will appreciate as quickly as your investments. Don't forget to factor in the rent you will pay if you decide not to buy.

For example, say you have $50,000 invested in a mutual fund that has returned 15 percent a year for the past five years. You see no reason that the torrid pace won't continue, but to be safe you assume that the fund will return to the historic market average of around 10 percent.

You would need the entire $50,000 for a down payment on a $250,000 home. If the home appreciates at a rate of 5 percent, it will be worth $388,000 in ten years. Thanks to leverage, you would have achieved a total return of 176 percent. That's the $138,000 increase that your $50,000 down payment bought.

If instead you had kept the $50,000 invested at 10 percent a year, it would have grown to $118,000 in ten years. That's a total return of 136 percent, less than you would have achieved with the home. In addition, you would have been paying monthly rent all those years. Say your rent was $800. That's $9,600 a year for a grand total of $96,000 paid over ten years. Subtracting that from the $118,000 invested leaves you only $22,000 ahead.

Clearly, buying would have been the way to go in this case. Now you see why I caution you against pitting your investment skills against an appreciating real estate market. Leverage is powerful stuff.

How Much You Can Borrow

If you've given thought to your housing situation and decided that home ownership is the right choice, you need to know how much home you can buy. Lenders look at two factors to choose the amount of money you can borrow. They are your income and your long-term debt.

Your Income

I've written repeatedly that you should spend no more than 28 percent of your monthly take-home pay on housing. But guess what? Lenders are flexible on that figure, and most will allow you to borrow money until your housing payment equals 28 percent of your *gross* monthly income, that is, before taxes.

So why did I understate the figure? For the same reason I recommend carrying no credit card debt. The availability of funds to borrow does not necessarily mean you should borrow them. I would much rather see you stick to my 28 percent of your take-home than rise to the 28 percent of your gross. You would save on every monthly payment and have more money to invest in the stock market, which has outperformed real estate through history.

If you followed the directions on page 12, you have already written your income on a blank sheet of paper. Add up your gross monthly income.

Take your gross monthly income and multiply it by 28 percent to find your maximum allowable monthly housing expense. For instance, if you gross $2,500 per month, you can afford a housing payment of up to $700. That's $2,500 × 0.28 to get $700.

The reason I can't tell you the size of the mortgage you can afford is that I don't know what interest rate you'll be able to find or how long you'll borrow the money. Borrowing for thirty years at a rate of 7.5 percent, you could get a $100,000 mortgage. At a rate of 10 percent, you could get only an $80,000 mortgage.

Here's a chart from Fannie Mae to give you a rough estimate of the size of mortgage you can afford. It shows monthly payments on thirty-year fixed-rate mortgages of varying amounts and at various interest rates. Find your allowable monthly payment in the body of the table, then see how much you can borrow at different interest rates. Keep in mind that the payments on this chart show only the amount of your principal and interest. They do not include insurance and other costs of home ownership.

Thirty-Year Fixed-Rate Monthly Payment by Loan Amount and Interest Rate								
Loan Amount	Interest Rates							
	6.5%	7%	7.5%	8%	8.5%	9%	9.5%	10%
$20,000	$126	$133	$140	$147	$154	$161	$168	$176
25,000	158	166	175	183	192	201	210	219
30,000	190	200	210	220	231	241	252	263
35,000	221	233	245	257	269	282	294	307
40,000	253	266	280	294	308	322	336	351
45,000	284	299	315	330	346	362	378	395
50,000	316	333	350	367	384	402	420	439
55,000	348	366	385	404	423	443	462	483
60,000	380	399	420	440	461	483	505	527
65,000	411	432	454	477	500	523	547	570
70,000	442	466	489	514	538	563	589	614
75,000	474	499	524	550	577	603	631	658
80,000	506	532	559	587	615	644	673	702
85,000	537	566	594	624	654	684	715	746
90,000	569	599	629	660	692	724	757	790
95,000	600	632	664	697	730	764	799	834
100,000	632	665	699	734	769	805	841	878

Your Long-term Debt

The other factor lenders will examine is the total of your long-term debt payments as a percentage of your gross income. They want to see no more than 36 percent, *including your housing expense*. So, if you gross $2,500 per month, your housing and other long-term debt payments should not exceed $900. That's $2,500 × 0.36 to get $900.

Your long-term debts are the ones that will take more than a year to pay off. The typical ones are credit card balances, car loans, student loans, business loans, existing real estate loans, alimony, and child support. Here's a simple worksheet to help you tally your long-term debt payments.

Long-term Monthly Debt Payments	
Debt	**Minimum Monthly Payment**
Housing payment	
Credit cards and department store cards	
Car loans	
Student loans	
Business loans	
Existing real estate loans (if you're not selling the property)	
Alimony	
Child support	
Other long-term monthly debts	
TOTAL MONTHLY PAYMENTS	

If your total monthly payments exceed 36 percent of your gross monthly income, you will probably need to pay off some of your debt before applying for a mortgage. Target your credit cards and car loans first. Nothing would make me happier than to see you trade the expensive bad kind of debt for the affordable good kind of debt. Besides, you'll get a home out of the deal.

Know Both Limits

You've compared your income to your allowable housing payment and to your long-term debt payments. Let's take a look at the two limits together in relation to your income.

This table, also from Fannie Mae, shows how much you can afford to pay each month in housing expenses and long-term debt payments. It uses the standard 28 percent of gross income for the housing payment and 36 percent of gross income for the long-term debt. Note that long-term debt includes your housing expense. So, if you make $30,000 per year and currently pay $700 a month for housing, you can spend only $200 per month on other long-term debt. That brings your total allowable long-term monthly debt to $900.

Gross Income with Allowable Housing and Long-term Debt Payments		
Gross Annual Income	Allowable Monthly Housing Expense	Allowable Long-term Monthly Debt
$20,000	$467	$600
25,000	583	750
30,000	700	900
35,000	817	1,050
40,000	933	1,200
45,000	1,050	1,350
50,000	1,167	1,500
55,000	1,283	1,650
60,000	1,400	1,800
65,000	1,517	1,950
70,000	1,633	2,010
75,000	1,750	2,250
80,000	1,867	2,400
85,000	1,983	2,550
90,000	2,100	2,700
95,000	2,217	2,850
100,000	2,333	3,000
130,000	3,033	3,900

Pay a Lot and Pay the Rest Quickly

Whatever portion of the home price you can't cover with cash must be covered by a mortgage. The larger your down payment, the smaller the size of your mortgage. With a smaller mortgage you will enjoy smaller monthly payments or a shorter duration, or both. So, as with a new car purchase, you should make as large a down payment on your home as possible.

Also, if you do not put down at least 20 percent on your home, you will probably need to buy private mortgage insurance, abbreviated PMI. Lenders require this because you do not have enough of your own money in the home to make them feel safe that you will not walk away from your obligation. If you put at least 20 percent down, they are fairly certain that you intend to pay your mortgage.

PMI is taken either as an upfront fee of about 0.5 percent of the loan amount and an additional 0.33 percent each year thereafter, or as a larger monthly payment until you have at least 20 percent equity in the home's value.

Getting a smaller mortgage and escaping the PMI requirement should be enough to convince you to make as large a down payment as you can afford. Now let's talk about shortening the term of your loan.

Half the Time, Twice the Savings

The most common mortgage duration is thirty years. That's a very long time and it gives the interest rate ample room to charge up a mountain of interest expense that you will pay to your lender.

Despite the enormous interest expense of the thirty-year mortgage, most people choose it because of its low monthly payment. It's a month-to-month world we live in. Throughout this book, I've written about the benefits of rising above the monthly rabble and seeing the greater picture of your entire life. I'm about to do the same with regards to your mortgage schedule.

Larger monthly payments for a shorter amount of time are far preferable to smaller monthly payments for a longer amount of time. You pay the same principal in either case. The difference is in the amount of interest you pay.

"Fine," you say. "But how big a difference could it be?"

Gargantuan. Would you believe that an extra $219 per month for fifteen years could save you $95,000 on a $100,000 mortgage? It's true, and I've got the table to prove it. Look at this:

Total Interest Paid on a $100,000 Mortgage at 8.25 Percent			
	15-Year Loan	20-Year Loan	30-Year Loan
Monthly Payment	$971	$853	$752
Principal Paid	$100,000	$100,000	$100,000
Total Interest Paid	$75,000	$105,000	$170,000

I find this table to be very instructive. With the fifteen-year mortgage, you'll own your home in half the time it takes you with the thirty-year mortgage and you'll also spend less than half of the interest expense.

Many people think that to achieve such convincing numbers they would need to shoulder a monthly payment that's twice as high. But you can see that it ain't so.

Thanks to the snowball effect of interest expense, the fifteen-year mortgage lets you own your home twice as fast and pay less than half the interest with a monthly payment that is only 29 percent bigger than that of the thirty-year mortgage. The fifteen-year mortgage is a bargain, folks. You should think long and hard about the benefits of financing your home for a shorter amount of time. •

You can see now why I recommend paying your loan off quickly. Here's a perfect opportunity to illustrate the benefits of not purchasing a new car. Almost any new car will cost at least $219 per month, most will cost more. If you opt for a used car over the new, you will free up the $219 each month. Putting that toward your mortgage will allow you to choose the fifteen-year over the thirty-year. Not only will you have saved the $20,000 or more of a depreciating new car, you will also have saved yourself $95,000 in mortgage interest expense. You never knew a hot set of wheels could cost so much, did you?

More Frequent Payments

Once you've chosen a shorter-term mortgage, you can reduce your interest expenses even more by making extra payments every year. Most mortgages require twelve payments a year—one each month. But there's no law against your making, say, fourteen payments per year.

In fact, most lenders provide a line on the payment card for additional principal payments. With your regular payment, you can enclose the extra amount and write it on the card. Because extra payments go entirely toward reducing the mortgage's principal instead of getting eaten up by interest expense, making just one extra payment a year can shave years off the duration of your loan. By now, you know that a shorter duration means thousands of dollars saved in interest expense.

All of that said, however, I refer you to our earlier discussion about the opportunity cost of buying a home. It applies to these extra payments as well. The value of paying an extra $200 per month into your home will not do as well as paying an extra $200 per month into a solid mutual fund or stock portfolio. If you're an investor, you may have much better uses for the money than a quick mortgage payoff. Only you can decide.

Same Amount of Money, but Faster

Even if you're not sure about making extra payments, you will be sure about what I'm going to explain in this section. You can save a lot of money by choosing a biweekly mortgage payment instead of a monthly. Your monthly mortgage remains the same, you just pay it in two installments. Instead of making a full payment once per month, you make a half payment every two weeks.

Lenders will not go out of their way to inform you about the biweekly payment plan because it costs them thousands of dollars in interest charges. The charming Beardstown Ladies show why in their *Guide to Smart Spending for Big Savings*. They explain that the monthly payment on a $50,000 mortgage at 8 percent for thirty years is $367. The mortgage would cost you a total of $132,078. If instead you chose to make a half payment of $183 every other week, the mortgage would cost you a total of only $109,996. You would save $22,082 just by sending half as much money twice as often.

When you pay every two weeks, you reduce the mortgage faster because you send money more frequently. The first half of your regular monthly payment arrives sooner and the lender can't charge you interest on it. Those little two-week advance payments save you a lot of interest expense over the years. You also

**Send Payments
Twice as Often**

make thirteen full monthly payments a year instead of twelve. Why? Because there are only twelve months in a year, but there are twenty-six two-week periods. Paying twenty-six half payments adds up to thirteen full payments. That's an extra month paid every year. These two factors—the more frequent payments and the extra payment each year—come together to shave about seven years and a lot of interest expense from a thirty-year mortgage.

Most biweekly mortgage plans require that the payment be automatically deducted from your bank account, which, in my opinion, is a nice convenience. Some lenders will also charge a small fee for the service. The fee is worth it. No lender is going to charge a fee so high that it offsets the savings in interest.

To recap, make as large a down payment as you can afford, choose the shortest-duration mortgage available for the monthly payment you can afford, then sign up for a biweekly payment plan.

Types of Mortgages

You now know several money-saving mortgage tips that apply to any home you're thinking of buying. It's time to look at the specific types of mortgages that are available to you.

Fixed Rate

As you may be able to guess from the name, a fixed-rate mortgage always has the same interest rate. If you pay 7 percent in year one, you'll pay 7 percent in year thirty and all the years in between.

Fixed-rate mortgages are simple to manage. The monthly payment never changes. That can be great when interest rates rise after you have your loan. If you finance your home at 7 percent and rates rise to 15 percent, you're smiling and telling everybody. But if rates fall to 3 percent, you're frowning and keeping quiet and probably calling the bank to refinance. More on that in a minute.

Points

With a fixed-rate mortgage, the interest rate is only part of the story. Points are the other part. A point is one percent of the loan amount. If a lender tells you that they have a $200,000 mortgage with two points, you know you'll be paying $4,000. That's upfront before you even start making payments.

The interest rate and the points are related like the front and back of your head. When one is up, the other is down. If you are willing to pay more points at the outset, the lender will reduce your interest rate accordingly. Of course, you can only afford to pay so much cash upfront, and a lot needs to go toward the down payment. Don't destroy your budget trying to pay more points, but pay what you can scrape together.

You can think of points as another form of down payment, and the advantages are the same. When you pay cash upfront, you enjoy the benefit of a reduced interest rate over the life of the mortgage. As you know, the life of a mortgage is a long and expensive one. Trimming just half a percentage from the rate can save thousands of dollars. If you hold the mortgage for the duration, you will more than recoup the cost of paying the points.

That's the general rule. The more time you intend to hold the mortgage, the more points you should try to pay. Think of it as investing in a lower interest rate.

Other Fees

In addition to looking for the lowest interest rate and paying as many points as you can afford, you should also keep an eye on other fees. With a purchase as large as a home, the word *other* takes on enormous dimensions. Whenever you see it printed on real estate documents, your eye should immediately convert the innocent-looking "other" into **"OTHER!"** and you should hear screaming in the background.

Application fees usually run into a few hundred dollars for processing the paperwork and evaluating your suitability as a borrower. Although you'll rarely escape this fee entirely, you can find a lender that charges less than others. Also, look for a lender that will return the fee when you are approved for the loan and close your home purchase.

The lender will want to have the property you are buying

Other Real Estate Fees!

appraised. That way they know in advance what they can sell the place for in case you default on your mortgage. The appraisal will cost you several hundred dollars.

You'll never completely escape the other fees. Buying a home is expensive, which is why you should only do it if you plan to stay for a while.

Keep alert and run the mortgage numbers through your calculator. Stop and think. Compare the total cost of each loan, not just one aspect of it. Ask for quotes on the same product. For instance, ask for terms of a $100,000 mortgage with one point at every lender. Don't get the terms of a two-point mortgage from one lender and a three-point from another. Never get pressured by anybody to move quickly. The home isn't going anywhere.

Be especially wary of no-point, no-fee mortgages. Remember that lenders are in the business of lending. That means whatever they toss out as bait in the upfront costs can easily be earned in spades from higher interest. No lender is being nice to you. If it looks like a dream, you're probably asleep. Wake up and find the catch.

Adjustable Rate

An adjustable-rate mortgage, abbreviated ARM, is so named because its interest rate can adjust. That works to your benefit in a climate of falling rates; to your detriment in a climate of rising rates.

The built-in flexibility of an ARM comes at the price of complexity and uncertainty. You never know from year to year what your house payment will be. Your budget becomes fluid, subject to the whims of interest rates and the adjustment formula of your mortgage.

Every ARM begins at an initially low rate. It's often called a "teaser" rate because you are teased into thinking that it's a very cheap loan and a good deal. As soon as the fine print on the mortgage allows, the teaser will become a fond memory replaced by a higher rate, perhaps as much as 2 percent higher.

The Adjustment Formula

The ARM formula is simple, but with a tricky variable that the lender chooses. Your rate is an index plus a margin. The index is a measurement of the prevailing interest rates of securities like U.S. Treasuries.

The margin is the amount that your lender adds to the index. It can be fairly arbitrary, whatever they can foist on you through colored signs that show smiling families around a new home with a low teaser rate printed on the roof.

For example, you might find an ARM that is indexed against the six-month certificate of deposit rate and uses a margin of 3 percent. If six-month CDs are paying 4 percent, your interest rate will be 7 percent. That's just 3 plus 4. If six-month CD yields rise to 6 percent, your rate will rise to 9 percent.

If you are looking at ARMs from two lenders, both of which are based on the same index, what's a quick way to tell the better deal? Just by examining the margin. If one lender adds 3 percent and the other adds only 1.5 percent, go with the one offering 1.5 percent.

The Adjustment Frequency

Once you have a handle on the ARM's formula, take a look at its frequency. That tells you how often the rate can change. Some can change every month, others every six months, others only once per year.

Along with the adjustment frequency, note any rate caps on the ARM. These exist to protect both you and the lender from a completely runaway loan. They limit the upward and downward change in rates.

A typical combination is to find an ARM that adjusts every six months with a 1 percent rate cap. That means the rate won't fluctuate up or down more than 1 percent every six months.

On top of the frequency caps, most ARMs come with lifetime caps. They limit the interest rate fluctuation over the life of the mortgage. For example, you might find an ARM with a lifetime cap of 5 percent from the initial rate.

Balloon Loan

A balloon loan begins its life like a fixed-rate mortgage. You're given a steady payment schedule. However, at a specified time before the mortgage is fully paid back, you owe the entire balance of the loan. Depending on the balloon mortgage, you might need to come up with the full amount in three years, six years, or ten years.

Sounds crazy, doesn't it? For most people it is. Some people choose balloons because they usually offer lower interest rates. During times of extreme inflation, balloons might be the only option for lower income borrowers.

Most people get another loan to pay the balloon amount when it is due. If they can't get another loan and can't pay the balloon, they lose their property.

My general advice is to avoid balloon loans. They're weird and dangerous and those two combinations can wreak havoc on an otherwise bright future.

Choosing the Right Mortgage

To quickly point you in the right direction, fixed-rate mortgages are the best choice for most people. They are easy to understand, easy to plan for, and easy to beat with frequent payments and additional payments.

Obviously, ARMs exist for a reason. That reason is a high interest rate environment. If you think rates are going to drop and you need to buy your property soon, an ARM might be the better choice. You'll have the uncertainty of a fluctuating payment, but hopefully the fluctuation will be downward rather than upward.

No matter what the interest rate environment, never take on an ARM if its maximum allowable payment would force you to tap savings that you do not have. Hopefully, you'll have a solid saving and investment program after reading this book. Still, it would be a shame to deplete all of it on a rising ARM. Look closely at an ARM's maximum payment and consider what effect it would have on your life.

Choosing the Right Lender

Since buying a home is probably the biggest purchase of your life, spend some time shopping around. Contact at least three lenders, preferably more.

If you feel overwhelmed, ask a knowledgeable acquaintance for the name of a good mortgage broker in your area. He or she will already know the best deals in town and will help you navigate the paperwork. For this service, you will pay an additional 0.5 to 1.5 percent of the loan amount. If the charge for the service is low enough, the broker can more than make up for the brokerage fee.

When doing it yourself, move past the biggest and best advertised banks in your area. Who do you think is paying for all that exposure? Borrowers. Find no-name lenders. Some of the best deals come from the smallest shops. Check the real estate section of your paper. Keep your antennae up at all times.

Finally, be sure to deal with a pleasant loan officer who will be with you from start to finish. You want to trust the person handling the biggest purchase of your life. You don't want to be their conquest, you want to be their partner.

Refinancing

If you follow my gentle prodding and choose a fixed-rate mortgage, be prepared to refinance if rates fall too far below yours. Refinancing is just the process of replacing your mortgage with one that charges a cheaper rate of interest. When you refinance, you can choose any type of mortgage, but because you are refinancing to benefit from a lower interest rate, it makes sense to lock in that savings with a fixed-rate mortgage.

The decision of whether or not to refinance is similar to the decision of whether or not to get a mortgage in the first place. It costs money to refinance, just as it costs money to get an initial mortgage. After refinancing, you will save on your monthly payment. From there, it's easy for you to see how many monthly payments you'll need to make before recouping the cost of the refinancing. If you plan to be in the home that long, then refinancing makes sense.

For example, say a refinancing will cost you $1,500 and your monthly payment will decrease by $75 because of it. Remember that you will lose your tax benefit on the money saved. So you're not really ahead the full $75 each month. You're actually ahead by $75 minus your tax rate. Let's say you're in the

**Run the Numbers
Carefully**

28 percent bracket. You would save $54 per month. That's $75 minus 28 percent, or $21.

Once you've figured your true monthly savings from the refinance, just divide the cost of refinancing by the savings to get the number of months needed to recoup your costs. In this case, $1,500 divided by $54 is about 28. It will take you twenty-eight months to start getting ahead on the deal.

That's two years and a season. If you like your little cottage and plan to be there long enough, proceed with the refinancing.

Student Loans

By just about any measure, student loans are a good invest-ment. An education introduces you to the world, helps you find yourself, and increases your lifetime earning power. Even if your own education is complete, you may one day help a child or other relative pay the expense.

I'm not going to spend any time reviewing the rising cost of college. I'm sure you've seen the figures by now. The only rele-vant point is that it's very expensive and getting more so every year. It has become a large enough expense that, as with a home purchase, many people simply cannot afford college without the help of student loans.

Even if student loans are the good kind of debt, it's better to keep them to a minimum or to get through school without them altogether. They are just one of four ways to pay for college. Here are the four ways in order of preference:

- Work-study programs allow students to take advantage of flexible schedules and on-campus opportunities. Work-study jobs provide good work experience for résumés and help foot the college bill. Every one of my college friends and I worked our way through school delivering sand-wiches, waiting tables, mixing chemicals, cleaning win-dows, and even selling Avon. The biggest coup of my college career was winning a grant to write a research paper on Colorado's Southern Ute Indian Tribe. They paid me the then-unbelievable sum of $200 per month. It was my first paid writing job and helped give me the skills I needed to bring these words to you today. Work-study programs are a fabulous way to pay for college. They teach lifelong skills and show students the value of the education they are pursuing.

- Grants and scholarships never need to be repaid. Grants are given by the government and private institutions to fund students in need, while scholarships are awarded based on need, achievement, or special circumstances. Everybody should apply regardless of income level or background.
- Investments that you make before attending college or sending somebody else are a good way to pay. Not only will you avoid going into debt, you will also have the opportunity to make more than the amount needed for college. You might be able to pay for college and have quite a bit left over.
- Student loans need to be repaid with interest. Because these loans are only available to students, the interest charged is usually less than that associated with consumer loans. Nonetheless, they do cost money and many people get in too deep. It's not uncommon to find people with advanced degrees carrying nearly $100,000 in student loans. They might not pay them back until it's time to take out another loan for a relative. Like all debt, student loans can be financially disastrous.

In practice, few people make it through school on any one of the four options. Most students combine the four to get by however they can manage. What I would like to make clear is that there are three very reliable ways to pay for college that you should exhaust before turning to student loans. I know several people who graduated from college with zero debt and no help from their parents. They saved before attending, applied for grants and scholarships, and worked while attending. One super-achiever in my class even graduated with some of his own money invested.

Incidentally, I am not one of those people. I needed to borrow several thousand dollars, which turned out to be fine. I got the education, got a good job, and paid the debts off as quickly as possible. If you do go into debt, keep it small and pay it quickly.

Let's look at smart ways to minimize the burden of student loans.

Student Aid and Scholarships First

Don't look into loans until you've looked into free sources of funding. Because college has become more of a necessity than a luxury, it's not difficult to find student aid and scholarships anymore. Even if you can't cover the entire cost of college with free money, you can cover a large portion of it.

And don't tell me that you don't qualify. There are students from families with six-figure incomes studying in college right now with the help of financial aid. I don't mean merit scholarships, I mean financial aid.

The formulas used to determine who gets the aid are complex. A dizzying range of factors is considered before deciding who does or does not qualify. Where you live, what you do, whether you're a veteran, and how many children you have—or how many siblings you have—all affect your financial aid eligibility. Everybody should apply for financial aid.

It's simple to do. You complete a stack of paperwork that you can get from high school guidance offices and college financial aid offices. The most important form is called the Free Application for Federal Student Aid, or FAFSA. Filing the FAFSA opens the door to a wide variety of aid, including Pell grants, college grants and scholarships, private grants and scholarships, Perkins loans, Stafford loans, college loans, and even work-study programs.

You submit the completed paperwork to the College Scholarship Service, abbreviated CSS. The service looks at your income, assets, and other factors including where you live, how much aid you qualify for from state and federal sources, and how much aid you can

Anybody Can Qualify for Financial Aid

expect from the college itself. The final number that CSS assigns to you is your expected family contribution.

The expected family contribution is the only part you will need to pay. If you never bothered filling out the FAFSA, you would be responsible for 100 percent of the cost of college.

After this very basic step of filling out the FAFSA, hunt for additional scholarships on your own. They're awarded for all kinds of reasons, not just academic or athletic achievement. There are scholarships awarded to students who write outstanding essays, play the cello, or live in a particular city or state.

The best way to search for a scholarship is to take an inventory of your family's history and examine the student's special skills. No matter how obscure you may find the skill to be, it might be worth some college assistance. Although my brother never found funding for his ability to snort a nickel up his nose and spit it out his mouth, I commend his efforts. The trick has certainly made for some entertaining moments at the cash register.

Once you've inventoried special skills and family situations, contact local community groups, religious organizations, libraries, schools, and trade associations. Don't forget to check scholarships offered by your employer or unions at your workplace.

Finally, check the Internet for possible scholarships. I conducted a search at www.yahoo.com on the word *scholarship* and turned up these promising leads:

- The Chick Evans Scholarship Program provides full tuition and housing for students who have been outstanding golf caddies and who graduated in the top 25 percent of their high-school class.
- The Harry Truman Scholarship Program provides $3,000 for the senior year of undergraduate education and $27,000 for graduate studies for up to eighty students committed to careers in public service.
- Donna Reed Scholarships provide four $4,000 scholarships for students with the highest level of achievement in the performing arts.

To conduct your own Internet scholarship search, visit fastWEB at www.fastweb.com. The site creates a student profile and searches more than 180,000 scholarships for free. With the profile stored, the system will notify you of new opportunities via e-mail.

Finally, don't forget the military. The three military academies—the U.S. Military Academy in West Point, the U.S. Naval Academy in Annapolis, and the U.S. Air Force Academy in Colorado Springs—provide four-year, tuition-free bachelor's degrees and a commission in the military upon graduation. Admission is difficult, but for qualified students, it's quite an opportunity.

The Reserve Officers Training Corps, or ROTC, pays the cost of tuition, fees, and textbooks and also provides a monthly allowance. Scholarship recipients participate in academic year and summer training while in college and fulfill a service commitment after college.

Look at Cheaper Schools

Just as you can save money on your automobile by purchasing a cheaper model, you can save money on your education by attending a cheaper university. A four-year undergraduate degree from a top-flight state university costs about one-third the cost of a private college. On average, public college costs consume about 16 percent of median family income, which is about the same percentage as it was in 1960. On the other hand, private colleges consume about 42 percent of median family income, up from 27 percent in 1960.

Naturally, there is a lot of pressure to graduate from name-brand schools. There's also a lot of pressure to drive new cars, and you've read what that habit does to your finances. With education, there seems to be less and less of a reason to attend an expensive private school.

When I worked in Silicon Valley, most of the heavy hitters came from state universities. Once you've landed your first job, the only thing any subsequent employer cares about is your on-the-job performance. I have never been asked about my education outside of my first job interviews at IBM. Even then, IBM was more interested in my specific courses and the projects I'd pursued outside of academia.

An Education Doesn't Need to Be Expensive

None of this is meant to downplay the quality of name-brand schools. They are superb institutions. But if you can save tens of thousands of dollars by getting a solid education elsewhere, isn't it at least worth considering?

If the prestige of a name-brand diploma is important to you, consider completing the first two years of a four-year degree at a cheaper school, then transferring to the name-brand. Many of the core requirements can be satisfied at state universities, community colleges, correspondence programs, and extensions. You then transfer to the prestigious school, complete the final requirements of your degree, and graduate with the revered diploma. Nobody will ever know how smart you were.

This is one of my favorite cost-reducing strategies. Paying $10,000 for the first two years of school, then $40,000 for the last two adds up to a $50,000 degree. All four years at the prestigious university would cost around $80,000. Investing the $30,000 savings at 10 percent for your forty-year working career would turn it into $1,360,000. You could use the money to construct your own library on the campus of your favorite university—the one that saved you enough money to retire rich.

Use Debt-Beating Payment Strategies

So, you've exhausted your available student aid, scholarships, and cheaper education options. You still need a bit more money to pay for the remaining college tab and you don't have it. Then get a student loan. That's what they're there for. You shouldn't feel guilty. As long as you've done everything to keep the loan amount as low as possible, then you have no reason to hang your head.

But remember that student loans are still loans. There's nothing magical about them. That means that all of the same strategies we've discussed with regard to your credit cards and auto loans and mortgage still apply.

Upon graduation, student loans should be paid off as quickly as possible. One of the simplest ways is the biweekly payment plan you read about in the home loan section of this chapter. If you can make two full payments each month, great. If not, two half-payments will still accelerate the payoff and save you some of the interest expense. As always, be alert. Don't aggressively pay off 4 percent student loans while letting 18 percent credit card debt linger. Don't forgo compelling investment opportunities to pay down a 2 percent student loan. But if your student debt is your only debt and you want to escape, attack, attack, attack. Pay all you can. Get it to zero and buy yourself a drink.

If your student loans charge a high rate of interest, consider consolidating all of them into a lower-rate loan, just as you would do with credit card debt. With student loans, there's a special program to help with this strategy. The Federal Direct Consolidation Loan program combines student loans into a big loan with a low rate. The interest rate is variable, so the payment due will fluctuate from time to time. Luckily, there is a cap at 8.25 percent as of this writing. To find out more, call 800-4FED-AID.

You don't need to work with the federal program. If you can consolidate your student loans at a local lender for an even lower interest rate, do it. Some student loans come with restrictions, but many can be treated exactly like any other loan. One source you should check is the Student Loan Marketing Association, affectionately dubbed Sallie Mae. While Fannie helps buy your home, Sallie helps buy your education. Sallie offers a bunch of different consolidation plans that will allow you to reduce your payments, lower your interest, or both. She also rewards you with a lower rate for establishing automatic deductions from your bank account. Give her a ring at 800-643-0040.

Your college years may create some of life's best memories. By following the guidelines in this section, you can spend your time remembering fondly instead of paying student loans.

Business Loans

If you run your own business, then borrowing money to make more profit can be a smart financial decision. Adding lanes to your bowling alley, more windows to your flower shop, or online credit card processing to your Web site can all bring more money. The idea is that you will have enough money to repay the loan and keep the rest for yourself.

But it's always best to finance future growth from current profits. Not only do you save on interest expense, you also test your mettle in the business you're running. Too many people think that more money will solve their business problems, but often there's more to the story. Increasing your profit margin through better supplier contracts and more affordable marketing can provide the extra cash flow you need to expand—and it will make the expansion more profitable once it's complete.

Of course, there are times when a loan is necessary. Most of America's largest corporations have borrowed money at one time or another. But, you're not General Motors. You're a small business, and small business can profit immensely from small changes requiring little or no money.

I know a florist in the Bay Area who wanted to open another flower shop across town. She believed that the demographics were right and that she had reached a stage in her business development to successfully manage two stores instead of one. She estimated the cost of opening the new shop at $20,000.

She applied for a bank loan and was rejected. She regrouped and decided that from her current cash flow she could afford a flower cart on the sidewalk. She purchased the flower cart, received a street vending license from the city, and began peddling flowers on the sidewalk in the new area of town. She sold them herself every day at lunchtime while leaving her main shop under the guidance of a trusted employee.

At first, the experiment was disastrous. She tried selling the usual arrangements for romance, birthdays, holidays, and funerals. Those were the mainstays at her original location so she assumed they would work in the new part of town.

But they didn't. The new part of town was dominated by big business. People in power suits walked past the flower cart without even a second glance at the traditional arrangements. So she changed her strategy. She scrapped every one of the traditional arrangements and made new arrangements specifically for business. She created a sign that read "Business Bouquets" and presented flowers as the perfect icebreakers and deal makers.

No Loans Needed to Sell Flowers

It worked. Her sales climbed until she cleared more than $1,000 per month profit from her street cart. She banked the profits until she had enough money to open a full-fledged business flower shop. To this day, it is thriving.

She tells me that getting rejected for the loan was the best thing that could have happened to her. It forced her to get creative and conduct market research on a limited budget. She didn't risk $20,000 to discover the needs of her customers. She risked a few hundred dollars. She learned with small amounts of money, changed her business plan, perfected it to profitability, then ran all the way. She never borrowed a dime.

She still uses the street cart method to test new cities. She considers it pollinating the fields of business. Some areas blossom, others wilt. But no matter what the outcome, it never costs her more than a few hundred dollars to test.

Look very carefully at your need for a business loan. Don't try money where creativity is needed. If there is a better way, find it.

If you do need a business loan, treat it as wisely as you treat the rest of your loans. Get the lowest rate possible, try to pay it back quickly, refinance at a lower rate if one becomes available.

Be careful when you approach a lender that you don't get talked into borrowing more than you need. Although most lenders are careful with small business loans, the fact remains that banks make more money on the same amount of work required with a big loan than with a small one. It's the same stack of forms and credit checks whether you borrow $20,000 or $200,000. Borrow only what you need, make your business profitable, and repay quickly.

This is a perfect time to show the benefit of borrowing from yourself. If you absolutely need a loan and can get a cheap rate on your home equity, consider that option. You will be able to write the interest expense off on your taxes. Also, consider borrowing from your investments and repaying yourself with interest. Some company retirement plans will allow you to take a loan against your own money. The interest expense is irrelevant since it all goes to you.

Finally, consider approaching friends and family. Be sure to write the terms of the loan on paper and stick to your promises. No amount of money is worth losing the people you love most. You'll derive great satisfaction in repaying a loan to a family member ahead of schedule. The goodwill and respect it creates are priceless. Conversely, failure to repay creates bitterness that can be irreparable.

Look upon borrowing from friends and family as an on-off switch. You either get it completely right or completely wrong. Make sure you get it completely right.

5 / Smart Banking

Banking has become as competitive as the grocery aisle. Print and radio ads push free checking, discounted loans, more ATMs, faster deposit clearing, and anything else that can get you to walk in the front door. It may come as a surprise, but the best bank for you is probably not a bank at all. Brokerage firms and credit unions are quickly fulfilling many of the basic banking requirements with better rates and cheaper service.

This chapter discusses the different ways to bank and makes sure you're on the right track.

Credit Unions Are Better Than Banks

Credit unions are not-for-profit financial institutions formed by people with a common bond such as working at the same company or in the same industry, joining the same labor union, following the same religion, and so on. For your needs, credit unions work just like banks, only better.

Because they are not-for-profit, credit unions offer higher interest on your deposits and lower interest on your loans. Most credit unions offer free checking accounts with no minimum deposit requirement. Most credit union fees for things like extra statements and bounced checks are cheaper than the fees at banks. In short, credit unions are superior to banks in almost every way.

It's hard to go wrong with a credit union credit card. Most are no-fee cards and you can automatically pay the balance in full each month from your checking account. You don't have to write a check or lick a stamp. Your balance will be paid before any interest accrues. No commercial bank would ever touch such a program. Commercial banks want you to carry a balance because they want to charge you interest. Credit unions don't mind offering you a good deal.

After reading this book, you will be paying your credit card balances in full every month. That being the case, you might as well make the process simple by having a credit union do all the work for you.

The only complaint I've ever heard voiced about credit unions is that they don't have a very large network of ATMs. That means you might end up using a commercial bank's ATM and paying a fee. However, credit unions have teamed up with one another to allow members of one credit union to use another credit union's ATMs free of charge, and vice versa. This maneuver seems to have helped the ATM shortage problem. When joining a credit union, make sure you have convenient access to an ATM.

How to Find and Get into One

There was a time when being part of a credit union was an exclusive boast. Not anymore. Almost every major organization is affiliated with a credit union. You might qualify just by living in your neighborhood.

The first place to check is with your employer. Most large companies have an employee credit union. If you are self-employed, check with trade organizations you belong to. Check with your church or synagogue. Check with civic organizations you belong to. Check with your relatives. Many credit unions offer membership to relatives of current members.

If you don't find any eligible credit unions, contact the Credit Union National Association at 800-358-5710. They'll help you find a credit union that you are eligible to join.

Once you are in a credit union, you're in for life. Even if you leave the affiliation that extended credit union membership privileges, you can keep your accounts at the credit union as long as you'd like.

Proximity Doesn't Matter

Don't worry too much about being close to your credit union's main office. With the advent of the ATM machine, you can continue banking with the same institution from across the country.

You Can Use Your Credit Union From Anywhere in the World

When I left IBM to strike out on my own in Los Angeles, I kept my Pacific IBM Employees Federal Credit Union account in San Jose. The interest rates were good, the service was friendly, and I paid my Visa card automatically from my checking account. Also, I had established automatic monthly transfers from my account to my mutual funds at Fidelity and Schwab. Changing to a new bank or credit union would have meant reestablishing the automatic transfers.

Years later, I still use the IBM credit union for my primary personal checking account. I make deposits and get cash at other credit union ATMs, and I write checks against the account as I always did. You may not be aware that you can have checks printed with your local address and phone number regardless of where your account is physically located. Merchants look at your address to determine if a check is local. They don't look at the bank's address.

Even though my credit union's main branch is located four hundred miles from where I live, I continue to use it as I always did. I don't anticipate changing it any time soon, if ever. Banking remotely is like swimming. If you can do it in five feet of water, you can do it in five hundred feet. If you can manage to bank from four hundred miles away, you can manage to bank from four thousand miles away.

Brokerage Firms Are Better Than Banks

If you're like most people, you use a bank or credit union primarily for your checking account. You might also have a savings account and possibly even a few investments with your bank. You probably carry an ATM card.

You deposit money into your checking account, then write checks and withdraw cash from the checking account. That's probably your entire relationship with your bank. Money in, money out.

That means the bank serves only as a holding tank for your money. Take a moment to think about that. You were raised to think that you need a bank to keep your money. That's just how it works, you were told. But when you boil it down to the barest essential relationship, it should become clear that banks don't do a whole lot for you. In fact, you can get the same money in, money out features of banking somewhere else. Somewhere better. Somewhere more sophisticated.

At the beginning of this book, I spelled out the path to prosperity. You should spend less than you earn, invest the difference, and protect what you have. Because you're going to be investing for a better future anyway, why not use your brokerage account to take care of your banking needs as well?

My two favorite discount brokers are Fidelity Investments and Charles Schwab. Both offer investment accounts that can double as your checking account. You deposit money by mailing it in a postage-paid envelope. You write checks as you have always done. You can sign up for direct deposit. You can even use a debit card to get cash at ATMs. You can get your credit card through your brokerage firm and have the balance paid each month from your account.

When it's time to invest in, say, a portfolio of mutual funds, you don't need to write checks or lick stamps or transfer money to do it. You simply call your brokerage firm— which is also your bank—and tell the friendly

Banking Features Are Available at Brokerage Firms

representative that you would like to move money from your core account to your mutual funds. Want to switch between funds? Same phone number. Want to establish direct deposit? Same phone number. Have a question about anything regarding your money? Same phone number.

Try that with your bank. In Los Angeles, the biggest banks in the area are notorious for nickel-and-diming their customers to death. Some of the banks charge customers for dealing directly with a teller. They charge customers for using another bank's ATM machine. They charge customers for calling on the phone for information that was available through the ATM. To top it all off, they are closed at night, Saturday afternoons, and Sundays. If you have a problem with your money on a Saturday evening, tough luck. You'll have to wait until Monday to deal with it.

If a bank is going to charge you for walking into its lobby anyway, why not just use Fidelity or Schwab? All your banking can occur at the ATM, through the mail, and over the phone. It's also free. Plus, you have access to your account twenty-four hours a day because Fidelity and Schwab do not close. If you want to talk to somebody about your money on Christmas Eve, just pick up the phone.

One of the biggest advantages to brokerage banking is the extra yield on your core account. You might have noticed that bank checking accounts don't pay very much interest. Many pay none at all, enticing you instead with no fees. True, they don't charge you each month, but they don't pay anything on your deposits, either. If you have a few thousand dollars sitting in your checking account, you might lose more money through unpaid monthly interest than you would have lost in a modest monthly fee.

With a brokerage firm, your core account is equivalent to your bank checking account. However, most core accounts pay the going money market rate of interest. As of this writing, checking accounts in my area are paying either 0 percent interest or less than 2 percent. My core accounts at Fidelity and Schwab are both paying over 5 percent.

There are four things you should be aware of before switching to Fidelity or Schwab for total money management:

- First and most prohibitive, you need to have a fair amount of money to make a brokerage account worthwhile. Both Fidelity and Schwab require at least $10,000 to get started. It doesn't all need to be sitting in your core account, but the sum of your mutual funds, stocks, and cash deposits must equal at least $10,000. That's pretty steep for a lot of people. Schwab also charges $5 per month until you reach a total account value of $25,000. After that, the banking features are free. Because these conditions change periodically, you should contact each company to find the most current offering.

  Don't feel bad if you haven't reached those rather steep requirements yet. It took me a few years to get there. With the lessons you learn in this book, you'll make it soon enough. In the meantime, I've got some other options for you. So keep reading and don't worry.

- Second, it might feel strange to be so distant from your money. Most people are used to going to the bank, filling out a deposit slip, chatting with the teller, and grabbing a doughnut on the way home. All of that goes away when you bank with a brokerage firm. Some people enjoy the convenience of using the ATM, mail, and phone, but many people get the willies.

  Now, both Fidelity and Schwab maintain physical locations across the country. You can walk into a branch office and talk to somebody directly, but you can't deposit money there. Remember, they are not banks. They are brokerage firms. So, while physical locations are available, you should know that most of your business will happen elsewhere. If that bothers you, then consider a credit union. I covered them in the previous section.

- Third, if you deal with a lot of cash, then brokerage firms aren't the way to go. As I mentioned, you can't walk into a brokerage office with $1,000 in twenties and ask them to deposit it into your core account. You can't even mail the cash in. Brokerage firms deal with numbers on paper and over wires. That's it. If you're a greenback kind of person, you'll need a more traditional banking arrangement. Again, read up on credit unions.

- Finally, if you make a lot of deposits each month, steer clear of brokerage banking. Many businesses make three trips a week to the bank with a bag full of cash and checks. Even if it's all in the form of checks, frequent depositing to a brokerage account will be a hassle for you.

While these four disadvantages remove many people from the brokerage banking scene, they don't rule everybody out. If you have an adequate balance of investments and cash, and you make few deposits each month, take a look at Fidelity and Schwab.

You can reach Fidelity at 800-544-8888, Schwab at 800-435-4000.

Get a Good Checking Account

As I mentioned before, the checking account is your primary need from a bank or credit union. Most banks pay the same amount of interest on their checking accounts. Credit unions will usually pay higher interest than banks, but the interest rate from one credit union to another will be about the same. Almost always, the distinction in checking accounts comes down to the fees you are charged.

Therefore, you should find a cheap checking account and manage it well.

Profile of a Good Checking Account

If you need to go with a commercial bank, start with the small ones in your community. As with loans, small banks will often give you a better deal on checking than big banks. Call at least five different banks to make sure you are getting the best deal available. You want to know several things.

- What are the fees charged on the account? These can vary from zero to as high as $10 per month on a personal account, much higher on a business account. Ideal: no fees at all. Almost ideal: fees for things that you never use anyway, like cashier's checks.

- What is the minimum balance required in the account? Some banks will advertise a no-fee checking account. When you read the fine print, you may find that it's no-fee only with a minimum balance of $2,000. If you can't keep at least $2,000 in the account, you'll be charged a monthly service fee. Ideal: no minimum balance. Almost ideal: a low minimum balance that you'll have no trouble maintaining.

- How is the minimum balance calculated? Some banks use a minimum daily balance method that requires that you have the minimum balance in your account every day of the month. If you dip beneath the minimum balance for a single day, you pay a fee. A much better system is the average daily balance method. It adds your daily balances and divides by the days in the statement cycle to get your average daily balance. As long as you averaged more than the minimum, you're safe. Ideal: average daily balance.

- What is the interest rate? You might as well make as much interest as possible on your checking account. Don't sweat too much over this figure. Your checking account is not an investment, per se. It's just a short-term container for money you use all the time. You'll earn your big returns elsewhere. But all else being equal, you'd rather have a high interest rate than a low one. Ideal: a big number. Almost ideal: a pretty big number.

- Are there any charges per check? Some accounts limit the number of checks you can write each month. Beyond that amount, you need to pay a nominal charge per check, which is a hassle and can add up quickly. Ideal: no check charges.

- Are there any breaks for direct deposit? Some banks will waive all fees if you establish a direct deposit of your paychecks into your account. If your employer can do it and you like the idea, this can be a fast way to a free checking account. Ideal: breaks for direct deposit.

- Is there overdraft protection? Some accounts will offer free overdraft protection. That means that if you accidentally write too many checks and exceed the amount of money in your account, the bank will cover the difference.

They'll charge a high interest rate on the money you borrowed, but it's usually cheaper than bounced check fees. Ideal: overdraft protection.

Manage It Well

It's not hard to manage a checking account. By following a few guidelines, you'll always know what's in your account. That means you'll never bounce a check.

Your Checkbook

Whenever you write a check, fill in your register first. It takes ten seconds. All you write is the check number, date, payee, and amount. That's it. Then you flip to the check and scribble it out. This simple, ten-second habit is almost all that needs to happen for you to know where your money is going and how much is left.

After you've got that down pat, start balancing your checkbook. It takes five minutes a month. All you do is fill out the worksheet on the back of your bank statement or hit the "balance" button in your personal finance software. Just in case your bank doesn't print a worksheet on the back of your statement and you don't use software, below is a painless worksheet to help you balance your checkbook. Have a blank sheet of paper handy for tracing items.

- Compare the check numbers you've written with the check numbers that have cleared on your statement. Write down any that have not cleared and add up their total. Enter the total on line 9 of the worksheet.

Painless Checkbook Balancing Worksheet	
Checkbook Register Balance Information	
1. Write down the balance from your checkbook register.	$
2. List any deposits or credits that appear on your statement but not in your checkbook register. Add up their total and enter it here.	+

Painless Checkbook Balancing Worksheet	
Checkbook Register Balance Information	
3. Add line 2 to line 1.	=$
4. List any deductions or charges that appear on your statement but not in your checkbook register. Add up their total and enter it here.	–
5. Subtract line 4 from line 3. This is your adjusted checkbook register balance. When you're finished, it should equal line 10.	=$
Statement Balance Information	
6. Write down the balance from your bank statement.	$
7. List any deposits you made that do not appear on the statement. Add up their total and enter it here.	+
8. Add line 7 to line 6.	=$
9. Enter your outstanding check total from the bullet before this worksheet.	–
10. Subtract line 9 from line 8. This is your adjusted statement balance. When you're finished, it should equal line 5.	=$

Your adjusted checkbook register balance should equal your adjusted statement balance. That means line 5 should equal line 10. If it does, you're finished for the month and you know the balance of your account. If it doesn't, you've failed miserably and need to seek help. It's people like you that have run up the nation's debt. Keep this up much longer and you'll be a sobbing guest on daytime TV.

Just kidding. You probably missed a check or an ATM withdrawal or a bank charge along the way. Find where it's missing and fix it.

Automate Your Life

To be really hip, try automating most of your deposits and withdrawals. If your employer offers direct deposit, sign up. On pay day, you won't need to go to the bank and stand in line. The money magically appears without your lifting a finger.

You can make the money magically disappear too. You need to pay your bills each month one way or another. Contact your phone company, utility company, mortgage lender, and all of your other bill senders to see if they offer free automatic deduction plans. If so, sign up.

With Automatic Bill Paying, You'll Never Go Through This Again

A lot of people shy away from automatic bill payment because they fear that their money could vaporize. Don't worry about it. You'll still receive billing statements in the mail and can contact the company about any discrepancies. They're not going to raid your account, anyway. The truth is, they've had your checking account number all along—it's printed on every check. If the companies billing you wanted to steal you blind, they could have done it long ago. Do you really think your signature is necessary for a check to clear? Nope. It's just a formality, left over from the days of yesteryear when you tied your horse to a hitching post in front of the bank. If you don't believe me, ask yourself how a debit card works. Just like a check, remember? You can even use it over the phone like a credit card. The money clears with no signature.

To put yourself completely at ease, remember that all account activity is reflected on your bank statement. You'll know if anything funny goes on by watching your statement every month.

I've enjoyed automatic bill payment for years. The convenience is terrific. I open a bill, glare at it for accuracy, write the deduction in my checkbook register, then toss the bill in the trash. The money is in the account. It's taken care of. No stamps, no long sessions at a desk with a pile of unpaid bills to slog through on a Saturday morning. And you know what? I've never had anybody take more money from my account than what they printed on the bill.

Give it a whirl. I bet you'll never go back.

Put the ATM on Your Side

Banking remotely at the automated teller machine presents you with both convenience and temptation. If managed properly, ATMs allow you to use better banks or credit unions that aren't in your immediate vicinity. Even if your bank or credit union is nearby, the ATM allows you to deposit and withdraw money twenty-four hours a day.

Therein lies the temptation. Fast access to your cash at the ATM can suck your account dry. It can also leave you without the faintest notion of where your money went. Few people mark cash withdrawals in their checkbook register.

The basics of using the ATM right begin with the cost. Many banks waive all ATM fees for transactions that occur on the bank's own machines. If you go to another bank's machine, you'll be charged. You might be charged twice, once by your bank for using a foreign machine and once by the bank that owns the machine.

To escape ATM fees, make sure you understand what machines in your area are free to you. If you're with a large commercial bank, you probably won't have any trouble finding suitable machines. If you're with a smaller bank or a credit union, you may have to search a little. Ask for a guide to local ATMs.

Once you've pared your transaction fees to zero, discipline yourself to use the ATM sparingly, at least for withdrawals. You can deposit all you want!

I've found that people who go to the ATM often are quicker to spend their money. It's a psychological thing. If cash is only a few buttons away there's no reason to keep an eye on spending.

Here's a convenient way to use the ATM. Figure your weekly or even monthly cash needs, then always make a withdrawal in that amount. Don't kid yourself into thinking that if you withdraw a smaller amount of money you will end up spending less. That's not how it works for most people. They withdraw $10, spend it, withdraw $20, spend it, withdraw another $10, spend it, and so on. They are the most annoying people in the world to go out with.

You can simplify your record keeping, tame your spending, and please your friends all at once. Make larger, infrequent withdrawals in the same amount every time. That way, you know that if you withdraw cash from the machine, then your account dropped by a

Don't Go Crazy at the ATM

set amount. You'll almost always have cash when you go out for the night, and you'll know that you need to be careful with it because you can't just swing by the machine for more money at any second.

For example, a friend of mine always withdraws $100 whenever he goes to the ATM. He sticks the receipt in his wallet and records it in his register when he gets home. The $100 lasts him a couple weeks. He spends less time at the ATM, less time keeping track of withdrawals, and he's always got cash to join me for a quick drive to the beach.

Compare that situation to another friend of mine. He withdraws just the amount he'll need for the day or evening ahead, then throws the receipt away. He spends all the money. That leaves him without cash, so he must always precede an outing by telling me, "Oh, darn, I need to stop by the cash machine." Is it any wonder, then, that on more than one occasion he's come back from the cash machine empty handed? His account was at zero. Wild ATM withdrawal habits are dangerous, and they can indicate a financial life that's on slippery footing.

Beware Bank Savings and Investments

Two quick words about the saving and investment ploys that banks will try to pawn off on you: avoid them.

When you're ready to invest, go to where the real investments thrive. That's at brokerage firms, not banks. Banks charge expensive commissions on investments that rarely perform as well as their no-commission counterparts in the brokerage world.

But where can you possibly learn how to manage your investments at a brokerage firm? I'm glad you asked. The next chapter has your answer.

6 | The Neatest Little Investment Primer

This entire chapter is condensed from my first two books, which you should buy to get the most out of this program. Those books are *The Neatest Little Guide to Mutual Fund Investing* and *The Neatest Little Guide to Stock Market Investing*. Together, they'll run you about $24.

This chapter will provide you with the very minimum you need to understand how to begin investing your own money. It covers investment planning, your tolerance to risk, and the fundamentals of mutual funds and stocks. The chapter concludes with an overview of how to ramp up from a no-investment program to a solid portfolio that leads to a lifetime of prosperity. You can do it!

Prepare to Invest

Investing is not difficult. You've been taught by full-service brokerage firms that you need their help—their very expensive help. You don't. Choosing the right mutual fund is not much harder than finding the best checking account. Once you've assembled a solid mutual fund portfolio, you can spend time studying how the stock market works, dabble with small amounts of money, then invest more as you gain confidence.

This section will get you ready to take control of your own investment portfolio.

What People Mean by "the Market"

You hear every day that the market is up or down. Have you ever paused to wonder what "the market" is? Usually, that phrase refers to the U.S. stock market as measured by the Dow Jones Industrial Average, often abbreviated DJIA or simply called the Dow. The Dow is not the entire market at all, but an average of thirty well-known companies like IBM, Merck, McDonald's, and Sears. The companies tracked by the Dow are chosen by the editors of the *Wall Street Journal*. The list changes occasionally as companies merge, lose prominence, or rise to the top of their industry.

The Dow is an index, which is just a way for us to judge the trend of the overall market by looking at a piece of it. The Dow is the most widely used index, but not really the best gauge of the market. A more popular index among investors is Standard & Poor's 500, or just the S&P 500. It tracks 500 leading companies across four industries. It accounts for 80 percent of the New York Stock Exchange. The Russell 2000 tracks 2,000 small companies across several industries while the Wilshire 5,000 tracks—oddly enough—around 6,000 stocks of all sizes. For foreign markets there's the Morgan Stanley EAFE, which tracks stocks from overseas. EAFE stands for Europe, Australia, and Far East. Here's the average annual performance of these five indexes as of December 31, 1997:

Index	Tracks	3-Year	5-Year	10-Year
The Dow	30 Large U.S. Companies	30.15	22.05	18.64
S&P 500	500 Large U.S. Companies	31.13	20.25	18.02
Russell 2000	2,000 Small U.S. Companies	22.34	16.40	15.77
Wilshire 5000	6,000 U.S. Companies of All Sizes	26.99	16.73	14.42
Morgan Stanley EAFE	1,100 Companies in 20 Countries	6.59	11.71	6.56

There are dozens of other indexes that you will encounter as you dig deeper into the world of investing. Each is an attempt to monitor the progress of a market by looking at a sliver of that market. One of my favorite indexes is the NASDAQ 100. It follows 100 top stocks from the NASDAQ, such as Ascend Communications, BMC Software, Food Lion, Microsoft, and PETsMART. It's one of the hippest indexes around.

You probably already use indexes in other parts of your life, although you might not know it. We create them all the time to help ourselves compare different values. For example, let's say you are interested in buying a new Dodge Neon. If one of your main selection criteria is fuel economy, how do you know if the Neon performs well in that area? You compare its miles-per-gallon number to the average miles-per-gallon number of other midsize passenger cars, such as the Ford Escort and the Honda Accord. After several comparisons, you know what is a good number, what is average, and what is below average. Notice that you don't compare the Neon's MPG to that of a Geo Metro or a Chevy Suburban. Those vehicles are in different classes and are irrelevant to your comparison. Thus, in this case, midsize passenger cars comprise your index.

As you encounter different market indexes, just remember that each looks at a piece of the market to monitor how that part of the market is performing.

The Three Assets and Their Objectives

There are three investment asset classes. They are stocks, bonds, and the money market. Stocks represent ownership in a company. When you exchange money for a share of stock, you own part of that company. Generally, if the company is successful and its earnings grow, its stock value will rise. If it encounters hard times, its stock value will fall.

Bonds are obligations by a government or a company to pay back borrowed money and interest by a certain date. When you buy a bond, you are lending money to the bond issuer. Each bond has a different quality rating that depends on the reliability of the issuer. The amount of time until the bond issuer pays you back is called the bond's maturity. It can range from three months to thirty years or even longer. You receive interest payments until maturity, when you are paid the entire face value at once.

The money market consists of investments that are a lot like bonds. The main difference is that money market securities have much shorter maturities than bonds. Some mature in one day! The money market is often referred to as cash. Typical money market investments include Treasury bills and bank CDs. Even your checking account is part of the money market.

There is a risk with any investment that it will lose money and the three asset classes have varying degrees of risk associated with them. Long periods of time make any investment less risky because it has a chance to recover from losses. For short periods of time, stocks present a high risk of losing money, bonds present a medium risk, and the money market presents a low risk. You'll read a complete discussion of risk, beginning on page 126.

Conveniently enough, there are three investment objectives to go along with the three asset classes. The objectives are growth, income, and stability. Most investors strive to achieve some combination of the three. Some people focus exclusively on one objective, others concentrate on one objective while devoting a portion of their money to the remaining two, and still others mix the three objectives evenly. Growth, income, and stability are like the three primary colors. They can combine to create any desired variation.

The three assets map perfectly to the three objectives. Stocks best achieve growth, bonds best achieve income, and the money market best achieves stability. If you're investing for a long period of time, growth should be your objective and stocks your main asset. If you're investing for a short period of time, stability should be your objective and the money market your main asset.

Let's explore each of these relationships in more detail.

Stocks for Growth

The growth objective wants to increase the value of an investor's principal. That is, if you send $100 at the beginning of the year you would like it to turn into $110, $120, or $150 by the end of the year.

Growth is usually accomplished through the purchase of stocks or stock mutual funds that appreciate over time. The idea with growth is precisely what flea market dealers seek: to buy low and sell high.

Bonds for Income

Growing Money Is a Pleasant Hobby

The income objective wants to maintain a flow of cash from an investor's principal. So if you send $100 at the beginning of the year you would expect to receive payments during the year or possibly at the end of the year. You could use the cash to purchase items or you could invest it. At the end of the year your principal would probably not have become as large as it would have under a growth objective, but you would have enjoyed a stream of income.

Income is generally accomplished by either purchasing stocks that pay dividends or by purchasing bonds. You could also invest in a mutual fund that purchases dividend-paying stocks or bonds.

Money Market for Stability

The stability objective wants to keep your principal from shrinking. It isn't concerned with getting you rich or providing you with steady income, it just wants to protect the money you already have. So if you send $100 at the beginning of the year you would expect it to be there in full at the end of the year.

Stability is accomplished by purchasing reliable investments from the money market like U.S. Government bonds. Even if the whole investment world crumbles around you, Uncle Sam will honor his obligations.

Almost everybody invests in the money market by selecting a solid money market mutual fund.

Comparing the Three

Here is a summary of each asset, its primary objective, and the risk that your investment will lose money in the short term:

Investment Asset	Investment Objective	Risk
Stocks	Growth	High
Bonds	Income	Medium
Money Market	Stability	Low

Understanding Risk

Every investment involves risk.

Even if you rubber band your money into rolls of $100 bills and stash it in a tire swing, you're not safe. You might forget which tire swing you hid it in. The rubber band could crack and let your money drift away on the wind, one bill at a time.

Stocks, bonds, and the mutual funds that invest in them carry risk too. The amount is different for every investment, which makes it easy to find investments that match your tolerance for risk. You might be a person who doesn't mind a daily price fluctuation. There are others who burst a blood vessel every time the Dow dips five points.

Everything Involves a Little Risk

Risk and Reward

The more risk you take the greater your potential reward. If an investment is so safe that it will take a war to lose money on it then it won't pay as much as the one that is a long shot. It's just like betting at the horse races. You might lose everything on a long shot but if it comes through then you'll be rolling in money.

With mutual funds, risk can be reduced to a science. By looking at the year-by-year returns and volatility of various funds and noting their investment objective, you can be sure that your money is going to a place that balances the right amount of risk against the rewards you expect to reap.

With stocks, risk is a bit harder to pin down. You can see how certain stocks have performed over time and how much they've fluctuated, but there's no guarantee that they'll continue behaving in the same way. There are no guarantees with mutual funds, either, but the professional managers try to keep the risk level appropriate for the type of fund. With stocks, you can estimate the riskiness by the type of company you are buying. For instance, large companies like IBM and General Motors will fluctuate less than startups like Netsanity and Biomedloss.

There are two flavors of risk with investing. The first is what everyone is aware of: that their money will shrink or disappear altogether. In investor's lingo, this is called a capital loss. People immediately think of this danger when they hear the word "risk." Scenarios for this range from owning stock in a company that goes bankrupt to having Cousin Wally skip town with the money he borrowed from you.

However, there's a different flavor of risk that can do as much damage. It's the risk that your money won't be worth what it should be over time. As you know, inflation drives prices steadily upward every year. If prices rise at 3 percent a year and your money is earning only 2 percent, then you're losing 1 percent of your money's purchasing power each year. Is that a safe investment?

Sometimes it looks like it. If you put $100 into a bank account that earns 2 percent a year interest, at the end of your first year you would have $102 in the account. It doesn't look like you lost money because your $100 is still there and has earned $2 more. But because of the 3 percent inflation cost, it takes $103 to buy what only $100 would have bought a year ago. And even with your interest payment, you only have $102, which means that your money buys less than it did a year before. Overall, you are $1 behind. Actually, you're even farther behind because you must pay taxes on the $2 interest.

Your investments should be risky enough to earn the amount of money needed for their goals during the time available to reach those goals. The key is time, which is what I'll discuss next.

Time and Risk Are Your Friends

Risk* isn't a bad thing. It's something to be aware of and incorporate into your investment strategy, but not something to be afraid of. More risk brings more reward with time. A solid rule is that the more time you have to invest, the riskier your investments can be.

That's an easy concept to understand. If your goal is to buy your husband a new pair of shoes for Christmas and he has expensive taste, you might start saving in July. Let's say the shoes cost $500.

---

*I use the term "risk" to mean day-to-day risk, unless otherwise specified. So when you see "risk," you know I'm referring to the risk that your money will shrink or that its value will rise and fall in short time periods.

It wouldn't be wise to choose a risky investment to store the money until December. The markets go through peaks and valleys and your six-month time frame could fall into one of the valleys. Your shoe investment might be worth half what you paid for it by Christmas.

Instead you should choose a money market mutual fund because stability is its objective. Money market funds are managed to protect your money and you might just be able to afford a pair of socks with those shoes from the interest you earn.

On the other hand, if you decide your husband can go barefoot for all you care and that the $500 would be better spent toward your retirement in twenty years, risk becomes your friend. You don't need that money for a long time and it doesn't matter to you what it's worth next month. In twenty years, since the market tends to rise, your $500 could become a small fortune. Do you care what it was worth ten years ago once you retire? Not really. As long as its general movement was upward and it reached your goals, you're happy.

If you chose the Christmas shoes money market fund for your retirement, you wouldn't have as much to retire on. It's true that at any given point along the path to retirement your principal investment would have been preserved, but in the end you would have less money.

For example, let's say you place $100 into a high-risk mutual fund with growth as its objective and $100 into a low-risk mutual fund with stability as its objective. Three months later, the high-risk $100 has shrunk to $90 while the low-risk $100 has grown to $102. One year later the high-risk $100 is worth $95 while the low-risk $100 is worth $105. So far, the evidence suggests that the low-risk fund is the better choice. That's usually true for the short-term.

Over the long-term, however, the story changes. At the twenty-year mark, your risky $100 is worth $700 and the low-risk $100 is worth only $300. See how it works? Over short time periods, the low-risk fund is protected from shrinking but only increases a tiny bit in value. In those same time periods, high-risk money might shrink or grow so that it is worth more or less than its original value. Over time, though, the high-risk fund should surpass the low-risk by a big margin.

Remember that there are two types of risk. What I've been discussing in the previous example when I write "risky" is the risk that the value of your investment will shrink. Given a long time frame, "risky" means something else. It means there's a possibility that your money will not be worth the amount needed to achieve your goals. Investments that are risky in one way tend not to be risky in the other. For example, if a mutual fund is risky in the sense that your money might be worth a different amount from day-to-day, it is probably not risky over long periods of time. On the other hand, a very stable fund that won't let the value of your investment fluctuate day-to-day runs a high risk of failing to increase the value of your investment to the needed amount over time.

The bottom line is that the more time you have to invest the more risk you should take. That doesn't mean you should grab your retirement nest egg and head to the nearest poker table, though. The risk should fall within your personal tolerance and good judgment.

Terms, Terms, Terms

In the investment world, people classify their goals by the amount of time required to achieve them. There are three general time frames: short-term, medium-term, and long-term. Here are their ranges:

- Short-term describes a time horizon of 0–5 years.
- Medium-term describes a time horizon of 6–10 years.
- Long-term describes a time horizon of 11 years or more.

How Much Risk Is Right for You?

The appropriate level of risk for you depends on the time frames of your investment goals, your tolerance for risk, your age, and how much money you have outside your investment goals.

With investment goals, time is the key. Remember the shoes

versus the retirement. The only real difference between the two goals was their time frame: six months for the shoes, twenty years for the retirement. But aside from the goals themselves, you need to consider how you feel about risk, how old you are, and how much of your money is at stake.

How Much Time Do You Have?

Take a moment to think about your investment goals. If they are a long way off, accept a higher degree of risk with the knowledge that in the long run it will pay off. For your more immediate investment goals temper that risk so that when the time comes to use the money, it will be worth what you want it to be.

Remember that the more time you have, the more day-to-day risk you can withstand. Little losses are compensated by steady gains over time. In fact, if you insist on too much stability, your money will probably not grow by enough to meet your long-term goals.

With More Time You Can Accept More Risk

Categorize your goals by their terms. Goals that are zero to five years away are short-term, those that are six to ten years away are medium-term, and those that are eleven or more years away are long-term. Within each term, accept more risk as you increase the amount of time. For example, say you want to add an addition to your home in six years and put in a pool in ten years. Both goals are classified as medium-term, but you should still accept more risk with the pool money than the home improvement money. Why? Because the pool money has an additional four years to grow. It has a longer amount of time during which to recover from losses and profit from gains.

Now, these risk levels are not scientific. It appears that the home improvement should have 40 percent less risk than the pool, but figuring out risk is not that precise. It's important to know this when planning long-term goals because there is a limit to the amount of risk you should take. For instance, a goal that is thirty years away shouldn't necessarily be twice as risky as one that is fifteen years away, and maybe not riskier at all.

How Do You Feel About Investment Risks?

It's okay to expect a life free of financial terror. You might have read everything so far about how certain investments fluctuate in value from day-to-day but will rise over time, and be squirming in your seat. Perhaps a recurring vision of an account statement arriving in the mail from your brokerage firm with a number lower than the one that was there last month makes your eyes water and your mouth go dry. You're not alone.

Financial advisors would say that you have a "low risk tolerance." There are psychological investment tests that ask questions like "Would you place your last $10 bill on a blackjack table in Vegas or in a safe deposit box?" Personally, I'd put it toward postage for cover letters and résumés, but that's not the point. The point of those tests is to assess your risk tolerance.

I won't ask you a bunch of questions because I don't think they're necessary. It really comes down to one question: How much will it bother you to see the value of your account fluctuate from day to day? You know that those fluctuations will even out over the long-term and that your investment will rise, but that might not be enough to comfort you in the short-term. Only you know the answer.

Even though your gut feelings are important when considering risk, don't let them outweigh your better judgment. For example, if you are nervous about losing money but are a twenty-five-year-old saving for retirement, you need to give serious thought to investing aggressively. Despite how you feel, the facts are that stocks perform better over long time periods than, say, a bank account. On the other hand, if you would place your last $10 bill on a blackjack table and are considering the same strategy for your retirement fund, you need to spend time examining the very real risk that you will lose all of your money. Though this is obviously an extreme example, there are investments that pose too much risk for certain goals. Even if you have a high tolerance for such risks, it might not be wise to expose yourself to it.

How Old Are You?

It stands to reason that the older a person is, the less time he or she has to devote to long-term goals. Therefore, older people should tend toward investments that present less risk. This isn't to say that older people shouldn't tailor risk levels to their individual goals, just that they should keep their age in mind when defining their goals. Just how much of a time frame does a ninety-year-old have to work with? Nobody knows, but it's probably safest to invest for the short-term no matter what the goal might be.

How Much Money Do You Have Outside of Your Investment Goals?

This is a good thing to keep in mind. If your investment money is a tiny slice of your overall budget, you can afford to up the risk a little because you don't have as much on the line. But if you are driving hard toward an important goal and are directing a huge portion of your income to it, be careful. It would be a shame to see that goal go up in smoke as your account balance goes down in flames. A quick way to decide how important this factor is in choosing a risk level for each of your goals is to ask how your life would be affected if the account were to disappear altogether. The chances of this happening with mutual funds and solid companies are quite low, but the question forces you to think about how safe that money should be.

Choose an Acceptable Risk Level for Your Goals

Once you've got an idea of the amount of risk you're willing to accept for each of your investment goals, you can search among different investments for one that suits your needs.

Mutual Funds

Your first investments should be in mutual funds. They are investments with training wheels because somebody else calls the shots. You choose the kind of fund you want and the manager with the best record; the manager decides what to do with your money.

What Is a Mutual Fund?

Mutual funds have become the choice of millions of investors across the world. Today you can select from over 11,000 funds—far more selections than you'll find on the New

York Stock Exchange. Americans have poured billions of dollars into mutual funds for goals like retirement, vacations, new homes, improvements on old homes, cars, business expenses, and higher education. In fact, one in three Americans invests in mutual funds and the value of all mutual funds combined is greater than the nation's bank deposits. So what is a mutual fund?

A mutual fund is a gathering of money from investors with a common objective. The "mutual" part is the common objective and the "fund" part is the money. When you invest in a mutual fund, you put your money in a pot with other people's money. The fund manager uses all of it to buy stocks, bonds, and money market instruments. In exchange for your money you're given shares in the fund.

A share's price fluctuates with the value of what the fund owns. So if you send $100 to a fund whose shares are worth $10, you'll own ten shares. If the value of the stocks, bonds, or money market instruments that the fund owns increases, the price of the shares increases and so does your investment. Say, for example, that the price of each share rises to $11. Your initial $100 will have turned into $110 because each of your ten shares is worth a dollar more. Of course, it works in the other direction too.

Throw Your Money in the Pot

The price of each fund share is called its "net asset value," or NAV. At the end of every day, the NAV is determined by dividing the value of a fund's investments by the number of shares sold. For example, if a fund owns $20 million worth of stocks, bonds, or money market instruments and investors hold 5 million shares of the fund, then the fund's NAV is $4. The fund arrives at $4 after dividing $20 million by 5 million.

Since the number of shares you own is proportionate to the amount you invest, your $100 returns the same percentage of profit or loss as a pension fund's $10 million. For example, if you place $100 in a fund that achieves a 10 percent annual return, your account will be worth $110 at the end of the year. A pension fund with $10 million in the same fund will have $11 million at the end of the year. Both you and the pension fund added 10 percent to your account's worth even though the pension fund invested a lot more money. That's the magic of mutual funds.

Open-end vs. Closed-end Funds

The most common funds are called *open-end* funds. This is the type I've been discussing so far. Whenever somebody sends money to an open-end fund, they purchase shares in the fund that are worth that day's NAV, plus a sales commission if there is one (more on that in the next section). An investor can sell shares back to the fund for the current NAV at any time.

The other kind of mutual fund is *closed-end*. Closed-end funds sell a limited number of shares. If you want to buy shares in one of these funds, you need to buy them on the stock market from somebody who already owns them. They are listed on the stock exchange just like company stocks and bonds. They also fluctuate in price and are worth what people are willing to pay for them—which might be more or less than their NAVs. The selling price of closed-end funds is not based solely on the value of the stocks, bonds, or money market instruments that they own.

This section shows how to invest in open-end mutual funds. They are much more prevalent and easily accessible to everyone.

Load vs. No-Load Funds

Among the thousands of open-end funds some charge a sales commission, called a *load*, on the money you invest. This can be as high as 8.5 percent of what you send in, which is a lot. For instance, if you send $100 to a load fund that charges 8.5 percent it immediately takes out $8.50 for itself and invests only $91.50 for you.

The remaining funds do not charge this load and are appropriately called *no-load* funds. These terms are muddied because some technically no-load funds charge other fees that aren't sales commissions. Luckily, the other fees and commissions are easily identified by reading literature from the fund company.

Some people assume that load funds charge a commission because they are better managed than no-loads. This hasn't proven to be the case, however. No-load funds have done as well as or better than load funds, particularly if you factor in losses from the commission. Remember that in a fund charging an 8.5 percent load, only $91.50 of every $100 is actually invested.

Does that mean that you'll get your money back once the fund posts an 8.5 percent gain? No. The commission was taken off the top of your principal amount, $100, which means you have less money working for you. The 8.5 percent of $100 is equal to $8.50 but against your invested amount of

Beware of Loads and Expenses

$91.50 it's only worth $7.78. The fund actually needs to return 9.3 percent in order to fully pay back the commission you paid. Not good.

No-load funds are a better choice. Why begin your investment at a disadvantage? A no-load fund insures that all of your money goes to work for you right away and that any returns instantly increase the value of your investment. You don't have any commissions to recoup.

Expense Ratios

Every mutual fund, whether the fund charges a load or not, costs money. The annual expense is called the fund's expense ratio. It's expressed as a percentage of the fund's assets. The average expense ratio for stock funds is around 1.40 percent. Bond funds are around .80 percent. Specialty funds like those that invest overseas or in specific market sectors tend to cost a bit more than the average.

To find what a fund will cost you each year, simply multiply your invested assets by the expense ratio. For example, if the fund has an expense ratio of 1.22 percent and you have $3,000 to invest, you will pay $36.60 by the end of the year. That's just $3,000 × .0122.

Naturally, you'd prefer to invest in mutual funds with low expense ratios. The ideal situation is to buy no-load funds with low expenses. One mutual fund company, The Vanguard Group, makes low cost its top priority. It manages the cheapest funds in the industry. The cost advantage adds up to considerable savings over long time periods. Just as debt interest works against you, so do high expenses.

If two funds boast comparable performance histories, choose the one with the lower expense ratio.

Why Mutual Funds Are So Good

Mutual funds are good investments for a number of reasons. For starters, they allow beginners to place their money in the same expert hands as the big guys. Corporate pension dollars aren't given any better treatment in a mutual fund than the scraped-together savings of a high school student.

It's convenient to invest in a fund, too. With postage-paid envelopes, a busy woman can write a check to the fund of her choice and have it on its way before she begins the day's errands. Or she can use a toll-free phone number to call the fund and have money transferred directly from her bank account. There's no waiting in lines to invest in a mutual fund.

Mutual funds are an easy way for small-timers to diversify their investments. It wouldn't be wise to risk all of your money on a single stock, hoping that it pays off. But without mutual funds, people with little money to invest would have few choices because they couldn't afford to own a bunch of different investments. They'd be forced to put their money in a bank savings account or CD where the returns are usually lower. In a fund, however, every dollar sent in is spread across many different investments, sometimes even international ones. That way if a single investment does poorly, the rest can keep the losses to a minimum. Mutual funds can earn more money than bank accounts but are safer than owning individual stocks.

Some investments tie your money up for long periods of time. You can't easily get at the money you've put into a house or withdraw from a CD before it matures. Mutual funds are liquid, meaning that investors can get their money out at any time. Some funds even offer check writing and debit cards. You should note, however, that being able to get your money easily doesn't mean that it's always wise to do so. Most mutual funds fluctuate in value and require time to smooth out the fluctuations. You shouldn't treat them like checking accounts.

Types of Mutual Funds

Mutual funds come in many flavors and they're getting more exotic all the time. You can buy funds that invest in small Internet companies located in Silicon Valley. You can buy funds that invest in generic big companies. You can buy funds that invest only in Japan. No matter what you need in your portfolio, there's a mutual fund that can provide it.

Stock Funds

Stock funds are the bread and butter of the mutual fund business. Because stocks provide the best performance over long periods of time, most people choose stock mutual funds for their lifelong portfolios. Anybody more than ten years from retirement should be invested entirely in stock mutual funds or individual stocks themselves.

Large Company

Large company funds invest in corporations that you know by heart. Most own shares of IBM, Disney, Merck, Microsoft, Intel, Boeing, McDonald's, Sony, and so on. There aren't a lot of surprises in large company fund portfolios. That might lead you to think that the performance would be boring and predictable. Not at all. In recent times, large companies have stomped all over their smaller rivals and have led the market during the raging '90s.

While you won't get the famed buy at $2, sell at $200 type of growth from large companies, you do get market dominance. Large companies are large because they're good at what they do. There used to be a saying in the computer business that whatever you do, don't compete with IBM. For years, people followed that advice because IBM would steamroll every small competitor in its sights. Then along came Microsoft and Oracle and a host of others who thumbed their noses at the conventional advice and went toe-to-toe with IBM. They've done just fine and have become enormous companies themselves, steamrolling small competitors in their sights. Now, it's not unusual to hear somebody warn that whatever you do, don't compete with Microsoft.

But notice that IBM is still around and still a major

contender. It didn't dry up and blow away when smaller companies carved out niches for themselves and then expanded those niches into industries. Investing in IBM has been profitable, very much so since its troubles in 1993.

So it goes with large companies. They tend to stay on top in one form or another. They have the best advertising campaigns, enjoy economies of scale, and aren't very risky investments.

If you are getting started with your first long-term investment, I recommend a large company mutual fund.

Medium Company

Medium-sized companies are a strange lot. I've read studies that say they are the most lukewarm category of investment. They enjoy neither the market dominance of large companies nor the huge growth potential of small companies. From my own experience, I have to disagree. Medium companies have been spectacular investments.

In a way, investing in a medium company is ideal because, contrary to the popular view I just shared with you, they provide some of the safety of large companies with some of the growth potential of small companies. Rather than being the worst of both worlds, they bring the best.

Buying a medium company would have been like buying Microsoft in 1989 or so. It was obviously an important company in a growing industry, but it hadn't yet become the company everybody hated for being so powerful. It hadn't yet become so big that it spent half its time trying to convince the Justice Department that it isn't a monopoly.

There was not nearly the uncertainty with Microsoft in 1989 as there was in 1985. Back then all the company sold was some obscure computer software called DOS—and how important could that be? By 1989, people saw how important DOS was and Microsoft represented a relatively safe investment.

How Important Could Microsoft Be?

Yet, it grew like a weed from 1989 to now. Today it's a huge company with growth prospects more in line with IBM and Hewlett-Packard. Its speculative days are over. But during that medium stage, it was a fairly safe investment with fairly certain growth prospects. That's why I like medium companies.

Small Company

Small companies are where you'll find the most impressive investment stories. These are companies that a fund manager can discover while they're still mixing chemicals in a basement or assembling circuit boards in a garage. Who wouldn't give their eyeteeth to buy McDonald's when it was considered a mildly promising burger stand? Who wouldn't jump at the chance to buy Cisco Systems when it was considered some kind of net-working shop?

I remember attending a conference in Silicon Valley in the early '90s and listening to an engineer criticize Cisco. He said they had plans to network the world. Preposterous, he claimed. Aside from the military and a few big businesses, who would possibly care about computers networked around the world? Of course, we all did. Cisco kept at it and was largely responsible for building today's World Wide Web. A mere $10,000 invested in the company when it was small is worth more than $1,000,000 today.

Those are the businesses that small company fund managers seek. Many of their stocks will die on the vine. For every Cisco, there are a dozen outfits lying dead on the side of the road. So the returns of small company stock funds will vary widely from year to year. But over time they can add a lot of spice to a portfolio.

When you have a solid foundation in large and medium company funds, find a reliable small company fund to boost your portfolio's performance.

Sector

Sector funds target the stocks of a particular market sector such as technology, health care, and home finance. You need to know what you're doing when you invest in sector funds because it's up to you to choose the right sector. The fund manager doesn't have the option of moving to a different sector of the economy if things in the fund's sector go south. You choose the sector, the fund manager chooses the stocks. As you can see, half the duty falls squarely on your shoulders.

Only look at sector funds when you have a portfolio of diversified funds. That will give you valuable experience with safer funds before you charge off calling which sectors are best.

Bond Funds

The only bond mutual funds that make any sense are junk bond funds. Despite what you read in the papers about Michael Milken and all the trouble with junk bonds, they are great investments.

The euphemistic label for junk bonds is high-yield bonds. That's because they yield more than other bonds. While many become worthless, most junk bonds perform well and pay their investors.

There's Nothing Trashy About Junk Bond Performance

The reason that junk bond funds are the way to go is that other bond mutual funds cost too much for what they return. Only junk bonds, with their higher yields, can earn enough to cover the mutual fund's expenses and still leave you with a decent profit. With other bond funds, such as those that invest in U.S. Treasuries, you would be better off just buying the bonds themselves.

Is it risky to buy the nonjunk bonds themselves? Not really. Most nonjunk bonds are very safe, especially those from the U.S. Treasury. Unless you think Uncle Sam is going to default, then U.S. Treasuries are safe investments.

You probably shouldn't attempt to buy junk bonds on your own. Because junk bonds occasionally default, you need a mutual fund's diversified portfolio to protect you from the losses of a few bad bonds. On your own, you won't be able to buy as many bonds as the mutual fund and might suffer a severe loss if the ones you own default.

So, to recap, invest in junk bonds through mutual funds and in all other bonds by just buying them directly yourself.

Money Market Funds

Money market mutual funds are like turbocharged savings accounts. You don't have to worry about them losing money, and they pay higher rates of interest than bank accounts.

I don't have any favorite money market mutual funds because they're all the same. They might differ by a few tenths of a percentage point, but it's not worth opening a whole new account for the tiny performance boost.

For your money market needs, just use the funds available with your existing accounts.

Global and International Funds

It's no secret that the world is getting more connected all the time. You might drive a foreign car and listen to a stereo made overseas. Your investments should capitalize on the potential growth available from overseas companies.

Among mutual funds, "global" means a fund that invests in U.S. companies and foreign companies. "International" means a fund that invests only in foreign companies.

Moving some of your money outside the United States is helpful for when the U.S. economy is having trouble. Just as it's smart to own several different types of companies in case one of them loses money, it's smart to own investments in several different countries in case one of them hits hard times.

Index Funds

In most years, 80 percent of the mutual fund managers will fail to beat the market as measured by the S&P 500. So you may wonder why you shouldn't just buy market performance. Thanks to index funds, you can.

An index fund's investments precisely reflect a market index like those you read about on page 122. It buys stock in all or many of the same companies that make up the index. The advantage to an index fund is that your return will mirror the index average—your return *is* the index average, minus fund expenses. The drawback is that you're guaranteed to never beat the index average. But, as you've seen, the majority of stock mutual funds don't beat the average anyway and their expenses are usually higher than index fund expenses.

That's the other advantage to index funds. They are very cheap to operate because nobody needs to spend time researching investments. In fact, computers do most of the work in running an index fund. You send your money in, the computer divides it evenly over the stocks of the index.

The Lazy Way to Wealth

All those savings add up to a lower expense ratio for you. How low? Remember that the average expense for stock funds is 1.40 percent. The best index fund, Vanguard Index Trust 500, charges only 0.20 percent. Paying one-seventh of the cost of the average stock fund to guarantee market performance is pretty compelling. In most years, the fund beats the majority of its competitors.

One last comment. Indexing works best in well-established stock markets where everybody knows everything about almost every company. That climate leaves little room to find something spectacular before anybody else. Thus, the index approach of owning the broad market works well. However, it does not work well in what are called inefficient markets, ones where there are lots of hidden opportunities. Small company markets and international markets are prime examples of inefficiency that allow sharp human managers to find the best places to invest your money. So, only choose an index fund if you want to invest in something large and well known, such as the S&P 500.

If you want to know more about indexing in general, give Vanguard a ring and request the company's most current literature explaining the technique's virtues. Vanguard was the first to offer indexing to everyday investors and is still the best at it. You can reach Vanguard at 800-635-1511.

In the interest of full disclosure I should mention that I have written material for Vanguard from time to time. However, that was only after I'd written about the company's indexing strengths in my first book, *The Neatest Little Guide to Mutual Fund Investing*. The compliments came first, then the affiliation.

Your Mutual Fund Portfolio

As you save more money, you'll want to manage a portfolio of mutual funds instead of just one. This section discusses how to assemble that portfolio and how to change it by knowing when and how to sell.

Allocating for Your Goals

As you now know, there are different times and different reasons for investing in the different types of mutual funds. You need to look at your goals and decide what percentage of your money to place in stock funds, bond funds, and money market funds. After that, you need to choose which type of funds within the major categories will comprise your portfolio.

It's not very hard, actually. That's what makes mutual funds such great investments for most people. In it for the long term? Go with all stock funds. It would be a good idea to own a large company fund, a medium company fund, a small company fund, and an international fund. I'd be willing to argue that if you chose a top fund from each category and continued investing 25 percent of your savings into each of the four funds for the next twenty years, you'd retire comfortably wealthy.

In fact, let's construct a solid long-term portfolio of stock mutual funds using the exact breakdown I just provided. We'll choose White Oak Growth Stock as our large company fund, Oakmark Select as our medium company fund, Baron Small Cap as our small company fund, and Janus Overseas as our international fund. Here's the portfolio:

Type of Fund	Specific Fund	Allocation
Large Company	White Oak Growth Stock	25%
Medium Company	Oakmark Select	25%
Small Company	Baron Small Cap	25%
International	Janus Overseas	25%

Although past performance is no guarantee of future performance, let's look backward at how this portfolio would have performed. Unfortunately, we've chosen some very young mutual funds without much history. But they are from fund families that do have a history in each style of investing. So, I'm going to show the past performance of a slightly different group. Instead of Oakmark Select, I'll use the returns of Oakmark Fund. Instead of Baron Small Cap, I'll use the returns of Baron Asset. Instead of Janus Overseas, I'll use the returns of Janus Worldwide. Each of these substitutes is similar enough to our target choices to make the glance backward worthwhile.

The reason I didn't choose these older funds for the portfolio in the first place is that I think the younger siblings will perform better in the future. But, if you would prefer investing in the funds that achieved the performance I'm about to show, they're available. Here's the average annual performance of the portfolio as of December 31, 1997:

Portfolio Performance		
1 Year	3 Year	5 Year
27.82	29.13	22.06

That's a market-beating performance for the five-year period, but not the one-year or three-year. Let's say the portfolio we chose could sustain a 15 percent growth rate for the next twenty years. Let's also say you invested an initial $10,000 and then $400 each month thereafter, $100 into each mutual fund. In twenty years, you would have $796,000. If you became extra thorough in your savings plan and managed to sock away $800 per month, in twenty years you would have $1,395,000.

You get the picture. Choose a portfolio of mutual funds that will serve you well over your time frame. If you're investing for a shorter period of time, you don't want the risk of an all stock fund portfolio. Perhaps you'd keep the large company stock fund, but choose a high-yield bond fund and a money market mutual fund for some of your money.

Surprise! You're a Millionaire

Keep in mind that the mixture of your investments should change as you come closer to your goal. For instance, if you are investing for retirement and it is twenty years away, you should go entirely with stocks as I just explained. When retirement is only five years away, you should change your allocation so that some of your money is in bonds and some in the money market.

As you save more money, you'll want to own more than one mutual fund. However, you shouldn't own too many. I have helped an investor in Los Angeles allocate her $3,000,000 among just five mutual funds. The portfolio has done remarkably well, with less volatility than the overall market. There's never a reason to own more than one of each type of fund. When you do that, you're only diluting your exposure to the best fund in the category.

For example, don't own three large company funds and three small company funds to feel safely diversified. The funds of a same type will tend to rise and fall together. You own more funds, but they're doing roughly the same thing. Choose the best from each category to keep your portfolio focused and strong.

When and How to Sell a Fund

You should watch your mutual fund portfolio to make sure it is on track to meet your goals. Compare it to the market, compare it to other funds you could have chosen.

If you own a fund that is not in the top third of its category at least one out of three years, dump it for one that is. You want to own the best of breed, not a fund that just barely keeps pace.

It's simple to sell a fund, so you can switch to another one. Just call your fund company or brokerage firm and tell them to sell it. If you want to move the money into another fund offered by your fund family or brokerage firm, instruct the representative to do so.

This is called switching because you switch your money from one fund to another. However, you're really selling the first and buying the second. It doesn't work like two bank accounts.

Stocks

Let me be blunt. This section on stock investing is not enough information to take you from zero knowledge to managing your own portfolio. Stock investing requires a lot of education and is dangerous when done wrong. Why, a person could write an entire book about it! Luckily, I did. If you are serious about investing in stocks—which you must be in order for it to work—then do yourself a favor and pick up *The Neatest Little Guide to Stock Market Investing*.

That said, I personally like stocks better than mutual funds. They provide greater focus so you can put your money precisely where you want it. They can perform extraordinarily well. They are exciting to watch. Owning shares in your favorite companies will make you proud. For people who know what they're doing and don't mind putting some time into their investments, stocks are wonderful.

Here, then, is an overview of stock investing.

Why Stocks Are Good Investments

You should know why stocks are good investments before you start investing in them. There are two reasons to own stocks. First, because they allow you to own successful companies and, second, because they've been the best investments over time.

Stocks Allow You to Own Successful Companies

Stocks are good investments because they allow you to own successful companies. Just like you can have equity in your home, you can have equity in a company by owning its stock. That's why stocks are sometimes called *equities*.

Think of all the rich people you've read about. How did they get rich? Was it by lending money to relatives who never repay? No. Was it by winning the lottery? Not very often. Was it by inheriting money? In some cases, but it's irrelevant because nobody has control over this factor. In most cases, rich people got rich by owning something.

That something might have been real estate. You learned the first time you watched *Gone With The Wind* that land has value and that owning some is a good idea. In most cases, though, people get rich by owning a business. School children learn about John D. Rockefeller, Andrew Carnegie, and J. P. Morgan. They all owned businesses. Henry Ford sold cars, Ray Kroc sold hamburgers from McDonald's, Thomas Watson sold business machines from IBM, Scott Cook and Tom Proulx sold financial software from Intuit. They all owned their companies. I sold magazine subscriptions door-to-door in school to raise money for the student council. I'm not rich because I didn't own the subscription company. See the difference?

I could have taken some of that money I earned pawning off another copy of *Reader's Digest* on Mrs. Klein and bought shares of the subscription company. Suddenly, I would have been a business owner encouraging my classmates to "Sell, sell, sell!" even if it meant they would win the portable radio instead of me winning it. The business they generated would have improved the subscription com-

"Sell, Sell, Sell!"

pany's bottom line and, as a shareholder, I would have profited. If all went as planned, I could have bought a dozen portable radios.

That's why owning stocks is a good idea. They make you an owner of a company. Not an employee or a lender, an owner. When a company prospers, so do its owners.

Stocks Have Been the Best Investments over Time

That's cute, you're thinking, but does it really work that way? Let's take a look at history and a few hard numbers.

The stock market has returned about 10.5 percent a year for the past seventy years or so. Corporate bonds returned 4.5 percent, U.S. Treasuries returned 3.3 percent, and inflation grew at 3.3 percent. Notice that Treasuries and inflation ran neck and neck? That means your investment in Treasuries returned nothing to you after inflation. When you include the drain of taxes, you lost money by investing in Treasuries. You need stocks. Everybody who intends to be around longer than ten years needs to invest in stocks. That's where the money is.

Investing in stocks helps both the investor and the company. Take McDonald's, for instance. It went public in 1965 at $22.50 per share. If you bought 100 shares, the company would have had an extra $2,250 to put toward new restaurants and better hamburgers. Maybe your money would have funded the research and development of the Big Mac, one of America's great inventions. Thirty years and ten stock splits later, your 100 shares of McDonald's would have become 18,590 shares worth almost $1 million. Both you and McDonald's prospered, thanks to the stock market.

How You Make Money Owning Stocks

This is really the bottom line to investors. The only reason you own a business is to profit from it. The way you profit by owning stocks is through capital appreciation and dividends.

Through Capital Appreciation

Sometimes called capital gains, *capital appreciation* is the profit you keep after you buy a stock and sell it at a higher price. Buy low, sell high is a common investment aphorism but it is just as legitimate to buy high, sell higher.

Expressed as a percentage, the difference between your purchase price and your sell price is your return. For example, if you buy a stock at $30 and sell it later for $60, your return is 100 percent. Sell it later for $90 and your return is 200 percent.

Through Dividends

As an owner of a company, you might share in the company's profits in the form of a stock *dividend* taken from company earnings. Companies report earnings every quarter and determine whether to pay a dividend. If earnings are low or the company loses money, dividends are usually the first thing to get cut. On a *declaration date* in each quarter, the company decides what the dividend payout will be.

To receive a dividend, you must own the stock by the *ex-dividend date*, which is four business days before the company looks at the list of shareholders to see who gets the dividend. The day the company actually looks at the list of shareholders is called the *record date*.

If you own the stock by the ex-dividend date, and are therefore on the list of shareholders by the record date, you get a dividend check. The company decides how much the dividend will be per share, multiplies the number of shares you own by the dividend, and mails you a check for the total amount. If you own 100 shares and the dividend is $.35, the company will mail you a check for $35 on the *payment date*. It's that simple.

Most publications report a company's annual dividend, not the quarterly. The company that just paid you a $.35 per share quarterly dividend would be listed in most publications as having a dividend of $1.40. That's just the $.35 quarterly dividend multiplied by the four quarters in the year.

Total Return

The money you make from a stock's capital appreciation combined with the money you make from the stock's dividend is your total return. Just add the rise in the stock price to the dividends you received, then divide by the stock's purchase price.

For instance, let's say you bought 200 shares of IBM at $45 and sold it two years later at $110. IBM paid an annual dividend of $1.00 the first year and $1.40 the second year. The rise in the stock's price was $65, and the total dividend paid per share was $2.40. Add those to get $67.40. Divide that by the stock's purchase price of $45 and you get 1.5, or 150 percent total return.

All About Stock Splits

A stock split occurs when a company increases the number of its stock shares outstanding without increasing shareholders' equity. To you as an investor, that means you'll own a different number of shares but they'll add up to the same amount. A common stock split is 2-for-1. Say you own 100 shares of a stock trading at $180. Your account is worth $18,000. If the stock splits 2-for-1 you will own 200 shares that trade at $90. Your account is still worth $18,000. What's the point? The point is that you now have something to do with your spare time: adjust your financial statements to account for the split.

Not really. Companies split their stock to make it affordable to more investors. Many people would shy away from a $180 stock, but would consider a $90 one. Perhaps that's still too expensive. The company could approve a 4-for-1 split and take the $180 stock down to $45. Your 100 shares would become 400 shares, but would still be worth $18,000. People considering the stock might be more likely to buy at $45 than at $180, even though they're getting the same amount of ownership in the company for each dollar they invest. It's a psychological thing, and who are we to question it?

Twice as Many Shares, Same Amount of Money

Mathematically, stock splits are completely irrelevant to investors but they are often a sign of good things to come. A company usually won't split its stock unless it's optimistic about the future. Think about it. Would you cut your stock price in half or more if the market was about to do the same? Of course not. Headlines would declare the end of your fortunes and lawsuits might pile up. Stock splits tend to happen when a company has done well, driven up the price of its stock, expects to continue doing well, drops the price of its stock through a split, and expects to keep driving up the stock price after the split.

Great companies like Microsoft and Cisco have split their stocks several times in the early 1990s. A $10,000 investment in Cisco at its February 1990 Initial Public Offering was worth more than $1,000,000 at the end of 1996. The stock didn't just run straight up 100-fold, however. It made four 2-for-1 splits along the way. It rose and split, rose and split, rose and split, rose and split until, voilà! 10 grand turned into $1 million. You can be sure that Cisco wouldn't have been splitting its stock if it wasn't excited about its future.

Remember that a stock split drops the price of the stock. Lower prices tend to move quicker than higher prices. Also, the fluctuations of a lower priced stock have a greater percentage impact on return than they do against higher priced stocks. A $2 increase is a 4 percent gain for a $50 stock, but only a 2 percent gain for a $100 stock.

More important than all this, however, is that splits are downright fun. I love it when my 100 shares become 200 and every $1 gain in price puts $200 in my pocket instead of the previous $100. I feel like a real pro when revealing my performance to friends and need to toss in the phrase, "split adjusted" at the end. I generally raise one eyebrow and lower my voice for effect.

Mutual Funds Are Best for Most People

I'd like to take a moment from our regularly scheduled stock program to point out that most people would do fine to get stock market performance only through mutual funds. I know that reading about runaway stocks gets the blood pumping and dollar signs floating in front of your eyes. But stay smart.

You don't want to take all of the savings you achieved by reading this book and blow them on a single poorly picked stock. It can happen. I've seen it happen.

Give yourself time to get used to investing. Don't feel pressured to open a brokerage account and start wheeling and dealing stocks. As I'll point out later in this chapter, you should at least start your investment career in mutual funds and graduate to stocks only when you're truly ready. Some people will never be ready to invest in stocks. That's okay.

That'll do it for the safety warning. Now, back to our stock program.

How to Evaluate Stocks

If the issue of how to evaluate stocks could be captured in this little section, we'd all be rich. Although evaluating stocks is quite easy, it's as much art as science. I can explain how to mix oil colors in a few simple steps, but it will take a lifetime of practice to turn you into an artist. So it is with evaluating stocks.

However, you need to start somewhere. It might as well be here. This section explains growth and value investing, then presents three stock classifications you should know.

Growth Investing vs. Value Investing

This is the most basic division between investors, akin to North and South. But, like North and South, there's a lot of area between each extreme that's hard to classify. Think of growth and value as being on a continuum. Most investors fall somewhere in the middle and combining the two styles has proven to be a great investment approach.

Growth Investing

Growth investors look for companies that are sales and earnings machines. Such companies have a lot of potential and growth investors are willing to pay handsomely for them. A growth company's potential might stem from a new product, a breakthrough patent, overseas expansion, or excellent management.

Key company measurements that growth investors examine are earnings and recent stock price strength. A growth company without strong earnings is like an Indy 500 race car without an engine. Dividends aren't very important to growth investors because many growth companies pay small or no dividends. Instead, they reinvest profits to expand and improve their business. Hopefully, the reinvestments produce even more growth in the future. Growing companies post bigger earnings each year and the amount of those earnings increases should be getting bigger too. Most growth investors set minimum criteria for investing in a company. Perhaps it should be growing at least 20 percent a year and pushing new highs in stock price.

Most new growth stocks trade on the NASDAQ. Growth companies you're probably familiar with are Microsoft, Intel, Starbucks, Home Depot, and Mailboxes Etc. Now you know what people mean when they drive past yet another Starbucks and say, "That place is growing like a weed."

Growth investors are searching for hot hands, not great bargains. They'll pay more for good companies. As a result, many growth investors don't even look at a stock's price in relation to its earnings or its book value because they know a lot of growth stocks are expensive and they don't care.

They just look at a stock's potential and go for it, hoping that current successes continue and get even better. They buy momentum, inertia, steamrolling forward movement. That's the nature of growth investing.

William O'Neil, a top growth investor and the founder of *Investor's Business Daily*, says in his seminar that growth investors are like baseball teams that pay huge salaries to top-ranked batters. They come at a high price, but if they keep batting .300 and winning games then it's worth it. Likewise, you won't find many bargains among growth stocks. But if they keep growing it's worth it.

Because a growth stock depends on its earnings and the acceleration of those earnings, the expectations of analysts and investors are high. That creates a risky situation. If a growth company fails to deliver the earnings that everybody expects, all hell breaks loose. Red flags fly left and right, phones start ringing off the hook, the stock price falls, reports shoot from fax machines across the world, and nobody's dinner tastes quite as good as it did the night of last quarter's earnings report.

Value Investing

Value investors look for stocks on the cheap. They compare stock prices to different measures of a company's business such as its earnings, assets, cash flow, and sales volume.

Growth Stocks Can Be Expensive to Buy

The idea is that if you don't pay too much for what you get, there's less chance of losing money.

Value stocks represent companies that have been overlooked on their journey to success, have fallen on hard times after more successful years, or are in a slump for any number of reasons. Hopefully they're on a comeback and the value investor purchases shares at the bottom of an uphill climb. Here's where value and growth are tied together. In both cases, investors want to buy companies with a bright future. The difference is that growth investors usually buy those companies when they're already steamrolling ahead to that bright future, while value investors usually buy those companies when they're still getting ready to start or are recovering from a tumble.

Using O'Neil's baseball analogy, value investors comb the locker rooms for bandaged players trying to rehabilitate. They don't cost much, and you might uncover a future star. Of course, you might get exactly what you paid for: a broken player or a broken company.

The value investor is a bargain hunter extraordinaire. From my interviews with professionals and novices alike, I gather that value investing is closer to what we've been taught from the time we were kids. What did you look at when buying candy? Probably which kind you could get the most of for your pocketful of allowance money. In school, you probably bought the package of notebook paper with the most sheets for your dollar. When relatives came by for the holidays they might have swapped stories of the great bargains or "steals" they've purchased recently. We're used to examining price with an eye toward value. It's no different in the world of investing.

Value investors pay particular attention to dividends. A company that pays dividends contributes to an investor's profit even if the stock price does not rise. That's comforting. Also, among big companies, the dividend yield is a great indicator of how bargain priced a company is.

Combining Growth and Value

Growth investing and value investing are not mutually exclusive. Many growth investors use some measure of value to time their purchase of growth stocks. Most value investors use some measure of growth potential to evaluate a troubled company's chances of recovery.

Growth and Value Go Together

Growth investors tend to get in when things are heating up and bail out at the first sign of slowing growth. Value investors tend to be very careful about where their money goes and let it ride out fluctuations once they decide where to invest. The contrast in these two styles is why I think value investing is more suitable to the average individual investor. Most individuals do not have the time or resources to monitor split-second changes in their stocks to act accordingly. It seems that conducting thorough research periodically and letting the chosen stocks do their thing is the best approach for most individual investors. That being the case, why go through the hassle of all the trading that accompanies pure growth portfolios?

These are my thoughts only and throughout this book I try to provide equal space to each style. I think most of us end up combining the styles in our personal portfolios, but with a tendency one way or the other. I've enjoyed excellent results from both growth and value investments, although I tend toward value.

Three Stock Classifications You Should Know

People always try to categorize objects in their lives to make them easier to deal with. If you hear the model name of a new car your first question is probably, "What type of car is it?" You know that sports cars are fast, minivans haul a lot of people, and trucks carry cargo. Stocks are categorized hundreds of different ways. In fact, from my interviews with brokers, planners, investment clubs, and people on the street, I'm convinced that there is a classification system for each investor. Our view of the world is shaped by our experiences and personalities, which is why no two people view the same stock in the same way.

Surprise! You need to know only three widely accepted classifications: the size of the company, its industry classification, and whether it's growth or value. I hate complexity as much as you do and I think these three classifications provide all the information we need.

Company Size

A company is either big or small. Next topic.

Although it's not that simple, company size is pretty straightforward. To investors, company size is called *market capitalization* or just *market cap*. Market cap is determined by multiplying the number of outstanding shares of stock by the current market price per share. So if your neighborhood magazine distributor, Mister Magazine, has grown like Jack's beanstalk and there are 4 million shares of its stock outstanding and they trade for $10 per share, Mister Magazine's market cap is $40 million.

Is that big or small? Compared to the kitchen table operation it started as, that's huge! From its $1,000 initial sale to venture capitalists, Mister Magazine has grown 3,999,900 percent. So from an initial investor and company founder perspective, Mister Magazine is enormous.

But compared to General Motors it's a pebble in the tire tread. GM's market cap is about $43 billion. That's 1,000 times bigger than Mister Magazine. As you can imagine, owning shares of GM and owning shares of Mister Magazine would probably be very different investment experiences.

So let's divide all companies into the five market cap ranges used by Morningstar, the most popular fund rating service, to classify the holdings of stock mutual funds:

Giant	> $25 Bil
Large	$5 Bil–$25 Bil
Medium	$1 Bil–$5 Bil
Small	$250 Mil–$1 Bil
Micro	< $250 Mil

In mid-1996, Morningstar looked at the fifty mutual funds in each category with the highest concentration in stocks of that market cap range, then measured their combined performance. Here's how the groups compared:

Market Cap	3-Year	5-Year	10-Year
Giant	14.72	12.77	10.39
Large	14.17	14.44	11.78
Medium	16.09	16.09	11.99
Small	15.19	16.83	8.7
Micro	16.45	16.56	11.45

Keep in mind that the figures are for mutual funds investing in the different categories. I like that, though, because it examines the record of real people picking stocks instead of the performance of the stock group itself. Your record will be better or worse than the aggregate of fifty fund managers, but probably not far off. A lot of people would be happy with five-year returns over 16 percent.

Industry Classification

You need to know what a company does to make money, otherwise you don't know which other companies to compare it to. Also, if you know what industry a company operates in you can keep an eye on that industry for trends.

In many cases, you'll know off the top of your head what a company does to earn a buck. You're probably aware that Boeing makes airplanes, Harley Davidson makes motorcycles, Coke makes soft drinks, AT&T provides phone service, and Dell sells computers. A lot of bigger companies make money in several ways, however, and you should know all of them. Philip Morris makes cigarettes, but it also sells food under the Kraft label.

You'll usually become aware of a company's business simply by getting interested enough to invest. If somebody mentions to you that Allamuck Corporation is going gangbusters and tripled in size over the past year, you'll probably look it up in the stock pages. Once there, you'll either rule it out based on a few key measures or get excited and want to learn more. If you call Allamuck for an annual report, search the Internet for Allamuck info, or make a trip to your local library, you're going to know what Allamuck does for a living.

Growth or Value

The last label you want to place on your stocks is whether they're growth or value. You read all about growth investing versus value investing on page 154. When you're examining a potential company, know whether it's increasing sales and earnings and is expected to continue doing so. That's a growth company.

Maybe instead the company has had a rough couple of years and its stock price is at an all-time low. After reviewing everything you know about the company, you might decide that it's not as bad off as everybody thinks. That's a value company.

Growth companies and value companies behave differently. Make sure you know which type you're buying.

Start with Name-Brand Companies

When you're first getting started with stock investing, start big. Just as mutual funds are a great way to learn about investing before taking the stock market plunge, large companies are the shallow end before getting in over your head.

Big companies are the name brands that make up your life. You know about Nike from your shoe closet. You know about Johnson & Johnson from your medicine cabinet. You know about Coca-Cola from your refrigerator. You know about Ford from your garage. You know about McDonald's from your trips into town. All of the companies that I just mentioned—

whose products are a regular part of your life—have been good investments.

Name-brand companies offer you the comfort of knowing that they're not going to disappear. I have invested in companies that literally do not exist today. Nor do my investments in them. But I have every confidence that the companies I mentioned in the previous paragraph will do business with your grandchildren. The companies may encounter difficult periods, but they will survive in one form or another and continue their leadership roles. That's a great comfort as you plunk down several thousand dollars on the stock.

They Might Stumble, but They Won't Stay Down

Similar to mutual funds, name-brand companies are fairly well-diversified investments. While they don't offer the diversity of owning entirely separate companies, they do offer the diversity of participating in several lines of business. For instance, you know that Nike makes shoes. But it also makes a complete line of sportswear and sells it from its own hip shops and from other retail outlets. Philip Morris sells Marlboro cigarettes, but it also sells Kraft foods in every grocery store. Eastman Kodak sells film to help remember the pleasant times in your life, but it also sells Bayer Aspirin to help escape the not-so-pleasant times in your life.

When one line of business suffers, a large company can compensate with better profits from another line of business. That's an added layer of safety that you won't often find among small companies. They tend to be one trick ponies hoping that the world really likes their trick.

So make your first investments in companies whose products you use every day and see advertised everywhere you turn. Then you can be proud to continue doing business with a company that you own.

Buy on the Dips

Once you own name-brand companies, don't worry too much when their stock value declines a bit. See it as a buying opportunity. That's one of the luxuries of owning large, reliable companies. As long as you don't need your money when the stock price is down, you can ride out the fluctuation and actually make money in the process.

With small companies, you don't have nearly the confidence that they will rebound. They often sink lower, one dollar at a time, a little more, a little more, oh darn you'd really like to recoup the little bit you've lost, a little more, and pretty soon they're worthless and you've lost your money.

Not with the brand names. Because you can be sure they won't disappear, you can also be sure that their stock prices will recover eventually. If you bought shares of Boeing at $50 and they drop to $35, don't freak out and sell everything to protect the rest of your investment. Put more money into Boeing stock at the cheaper price. Let's say you pick up another 100 shares at $35. When the stock recovers to your initial buy price of $50, you not only recovered everything that you'd lost on paper, you made an additional $1,500 profit.

Watch your name-brand stocks and buy more when they dip.

Stay the Course

There is one thing that you can definitely count on in the stock market. It will fluctuate. Sometimes up and sometimes down, but it will always fluctuate and so will the value of your investments.

When it happens, you will be tempted to get out while you've still got some money. Don't do it. If you don't have enough time to ride out market fluctuations, then you shouldn't be in the stock market. If you do have time, then ride them.

Ignore the Gurus

Whatever your inclination, don't spend any time listening to so-called market gurus. They're also called experts, analysts, forecasters, pundits, and soothsayers. By and large they don't know anything more than what you and I know. Always keep in mind the market forecast of J. P. Morgan, "It will fluctuate." That's about all there is to say and it's never wrong.

Ben Graham, one of the fathers of modern investing, said that Mr. Market is like a manic depressive. Sometimes he's happy and sometimes he's sad and it's anyone's guess as to what he'll be next month or next year. Did you catch that last part? It's *anyone's* guess. The only difference between your guess and the guess of a guru is that you don't get paid for yours.

You've probably heard ·about the major pundits. There's Elaine Garzarelli, who correctly predicted the crash of 1987. Her days in the sun ended in 1996 when she told people to get out of the market after a 400-point Dow slide—just as it started to rise again.

There's Michael Metz, the chief investment strategist for Oppenheimer and Company, who warned investors of a stock market backslide in early 1995. The market gained 37.5 percent that year. So he repeated his warning in 1996. The market gained 23 percent. He repeated his warning a third time in 1997. The market gained 33 percent.

There's Ken and Daria Dolan, America's favorite financial couple, who said, "By the end of 1995, mutual funds will be the most despised investments." The average stock mutual fund gained 31 percent in 1995.

There's Barton Biggs, Morgan Stanley's global strategist who told everyone at the end of 1995 that a cyclical bear market would wipe us out and that aggressive mutual funds would be the worst investments. The average stock mutual fund gained 19.5 percent in 1996.

Are you convinced that your guess is as good as theirs? The worst thing that could happen is that you'd be wrong. Heck, that seems to be a requirement among gurus these days.

Forecasting or Marketing?

The truth, of course, is that none of the forecasts coming from newsletter writers and other guru types are intended to make you money. They're intended to sell a product. Nothing gets attention better than a panic-inducing outlook. If you're in the business of calling the market, it's always safer to call for it to crash than to soar. Here's why: If you call for it to crash and it doesn't, nobody is very upset because they made money when you said they wouldn't. But if you call for the market to soar and instead it crashes, watch out. Everybody who listened to you lost money because of your call and they'll be slow to forget it.

Following Elaine Garzarelli's July 23, 1996, sell alert, the *New York Times* wrote, "The most shrill voices often belong to people not backed by a major institution. Some attract attention by staking out extreme positions and by then being the quickest and the loudest to say they were right. And the prospect of a bear market is particularly enticing to them because it offers a once-in-a-market-cycle opportunity to seal their fortune as market gurus. A well-timed market call could mean huge rewards as a highly paid investment strategist, a sought-after portfolio manager or a popular newsletter writer."

Treat almost all market forecasts as infomercials. There's a lot of material there and some of it might be useful to you, but it's there to move a product. Your bottom line is never as important to the forecaster as his or her bottom line. The major institutions like Morgan Stanley, Oppenheimer, and Merrill Lynch are selling products as well. They don't sell newsletters, but they sell managed accounts. If one of their analysts scares the daylights out of everybody, people might want to open accounts there where they incorrectly assume they'll be taken care of through the impending disaster.

We Could All Be Gurus

If you think about it, somebody's always going to be right. On any given day of the year, somebody is calling for the market to rise like a star and some other clown is calling for it to fall like a rock. One of them is going to be right eventually and when he or she is, it'll be printed on the outside of envelopes and at the top of marketing fliers. All that really happened is that the guru won a coin toss. It could have just as easily been the other guy.

Why listen to gurus? Your guess is as good as theirs. You knew going into the market that it has its good days and bad, good years and bad, indeed it has good decades and bad. If you know your time frame and have a clear target in mind for each of your investments, you'll be fine. Long-term money can ride out fluctuations and short-term money should be protected. That's all anybody can ever know.

Be Careful of Who You Listen To

You Knew This Was Coming, so Why Worry?

From all your reading to this point, you should be well aware that the market fluctuates. Always, friend. It won't stop because your money has finally arrived there. In fact, from your vantage point it will start fluctuating more than ever. It won't, of course, but somehow the numbers mean more when it's your money on the line.

Don't worry about it. Money you invest in stocks shouldn't be money you need for groceries next month or college tuition next year. If you define your goals clearly and invest by those goals, you're geared for whatever comes. The money you *do* need for groceries is safely deposited in a bank account. The money you *do* need for college tuition next year might also be in a bank account or perhaps a conservative mutual fund. The money you have earmarked for long-term goals such as retirement or a new home can withstand any short-term market fluctuations. It's a science. The more time you have, the more risk you can take. The less time you have, the less risk you can take.

Your First Investment Account

To invest, you'll need to open an account with a discount brokerage firm. It's very easy to do so, easier in fact than opening a bank account. You can do it all through the mail at your convenience. Most firms will open your account with less than $1,000.

Discount Brokerage Firms

If you're going to invest only in mutual funds for a while, I recommend that you open an account at either Fidelity Investments (800-544-8666) or Charles Schwab (800-435-4000). Each firm offers hundreds of no-load mutual funds with no transaction fees. That means you can assemble a portfolio of the best funds from many different fund companies in a single account. You'll receive one statement each month, have one phone number to call for assistance, and receive one tax form at the end of the year.

Choosing is not easy. The choice of funds overlaps between the two firms, but each offers a handful of funds that the other does not. One of the most obvious differences is that Fidelity's own broad range of funds are available only through an account at Fidelity. You'll need to peruse each company's listing of available funds and decide which is most likely to suit your needs. If you have enough money and can't decide between Fidelity and Schwab, you can always open an account at each firm.

When you have an account with Fidelity or Schwab, you can still contact individual fund companies for more information, such as prospectuses and annual reports. If you decide to invest in one of the funds, you can do it through your Fidelity or Schwab account for free if the fund is offered through the no-transaction fee network. You will receive a list of participating funds from Fidelity and Schwab when you open your account. You can request a new list at any time by simply calling either company. In fact, you don't need to have an account to receive a list. You can call right now if you want.

Both Fidelity and Schwab train some of the best phone representatives I have ever dealt with. Far from the experience you've come to dread when calling your state's motor vehicle department or the IRS, calling Fidelity and Schwab is as pleasant as business gets. The representatives are friendly, competent, and thorough. As you build wealth, it is very satisfying to move your money around with a simple phone call. Once you've established links between your checking account and your brokerage account, you can call anytime to transfer money between the two. It's heady stuff when you first experience it.

I remember the day I watched a formerly poor friend of mine transfer $20,000 from her checking account to her brokerage account. She had worked hard for years to overcome her debts, tame her expenses, and begin a savings and investment program. She also built her publicity firm into a strong business.

After paying off her debts, she saved $10,000 and opened an account at Fidelity. She chose four mutual funds and automatically invested in each one every month. When the lump sum payment for two big clients came in, she decided it was too much to leave in her low-interest checking account. She asked for my help in moving the money to Fidelity. I sat with her as she called Fidelity, got a representative on the phone, and simply said, "I would like to transfer $20,000 from my checking account to a money market mutual fund." In less than a minute, the call was

A Joyful Call to Make

complete. She hung up the phone and just smiled.

That's how pleasant good money management can be. That's what you're striving for, and that's how both Fidelity and Schwab can help you.

Now, if you ever decide to invest in stocks on your own, you can do it at Fidelity and Schwab. However, there are cheaper alternatives on the Internet. Because an Internet broker's overhead is so low, their stock commissions are dirt cheap. At Fidelity and Schwab, you'll pay around $30 for a single stock trade. At an Internet broker, such as Ameritrade and E*Trade, you'll pay less than $15 in most cases.

But, if you do very little stock trading—which is probably the right choice for most people, especially if you're just learning to invest—it's not worth opening a separate account at an Internet broker. Do your first stock trades over the phone or on the Web through your existing account at either Fidelity or Schwab. The convenience of keeping your entire investment portfolio consolidated in a single account will probably outweigh the small savings you would achieve by opening an additional account at an Internet broker. If you ever start making more stock trades than mutual fund trades, you can always move the stock portion of your portfolio to an Internet broker and begin trading at the lower prices.

Some Smart Choices

Regardless of where you open your brokerage account, there are two strategies I would like to see you practice.

Reinvest Dividends

When you invest in either mutual funds or stocks, you will periodically receive payments from your investment. With mutual funds, the payments are usually profits received from the fund's stock trades, dividends, or interest. With stocks, any payments will come from dividends that your stocks declare.

You should check the box on your brokerage account application that specifies to reinvest all dividends and payments. That way, all profits from your investments will automatically be reinvested for future profits. There's no point in receiving a check that you deposit and spend. Your account will grow faster if you keep plowing all of its proceeds back into the investment that produced the profits in the first place.

You'll never miss the money and you'll get rich that much quicker.

Dollar-Cost Average

Once you begin your investment program, you should contribute to it regularly. By doing so you'll develop a habit of saving and it also makes for one of the simplest and most effective investment strategies.

When you invest the same amount of money on a regular basis, the average cost of your shares usually decreases. This is called dollar-cost averaging. It forces your money to buy more shares when the price is lower and fewer shares when the price is higher. Look at this six-month investment program:

Date	Investment	Price per Share	Shares Purchased
January 15	$100	$25	4
February 15	$100	$20	5
March 15	$100	$10	10
April 15	$100	$15	6.7
May 15	$100	$25	4
June 15	$100	$30	3.3
Totals	$600	$20.83 (average)	33

Average Market Price per Share	$20.83
Average Price Paid per Share	$18.18
Average Savings per Share	$2.65

This investor sent $100 on the fifteenth of each month regardless of the investment's price. At the end of six months, he calculated the average price he paid per share by dividing his $600 investment by the 33 shares he owns. In the end he saved an average of $2.65 on each share he purchased just by sending the same amount of money on a regular basis. Notice that this plan works whether he was buying shares in a mutual fund or shares of stock.

Dollar-cost averaging doesn't guarantee anything. It's possible to continue saving money per share as the price drops straight into the dirt. Sure you would have bought more shares when the price was down but the fact still remains that the shares are worthless.

Nonetheless, dollar-cost averaging is the simplest way for investors to build wealth over time. No investment strategy can guarantee good results but dollar-cost averaging is certainly preferable to guessing the best time to invest. In most cases dollar-cost averaging will lower the average price per share and it is less risky than moving large amounts of money all at once.

As I've mentioned several times, you can automate a schedule of regular investing into your mutual funds. Both Fidelity and Schwab will send you a simple form that you return to them with a voided check and the schedule that works best for you. If you ever want to skip a month, send more money one month, or change your program entirely, one phone call does it all.

I don't know of any brokerage firms that allow you to automate investments into individual stocks, but some company stock purchase plans allow it. For instance, when I worked at IBM, I specified to automatically invest 10 percent of every paycheck in IBM stock. When I left the company, I transferred all 5 million shares to Ameritrade and traded them as I would any other shares of stock. I'm kidding about the number of shares, but the transfer really did happen.

Your Path to Investment Prosperity

First, of course, you need to use the beginning of this book to get your debt and spending under control. When that frees up some cash, you need to establish your emergency fund of three to six months' worth of income. When that's finished, start directing money into the retirement plans that are available to you at work. If you're self-employed, make sure you are contributing as much as you can to an IRA or SEP-IRA (more on both in the next chapter).

Only after all of that is taken care of should you even consider investing in mutual funds and stocks for nonretirement goals. This is the top of the pyramid, the final stone that places the magic gem in the light of prosperity. But it will not reach the light without the supporting stones below. Don't be premature. Take care of the less exciting stones first because they are actually more important.

But once you are ready to invest in mutual funds and stocks for nonretirement, the good times are gonna roll. This chapter shows the steps to take.

Save the Minimum Amounts Needed

Most mutual funds require $2,500 to get started, but some require only $1,000. I recommend saving $1,000 and then opening an account at Fidelity or Schwab. If you do not have enough for the mutual fund you want, automate your savings plan to transfer whatever you can afford each month from your checking account to your brokerage account.

Build a Core of Mutual Funds

When you have the amount needed to invest in your favorite fund, call up and do it! Keep investing into that fund until you have enough for two funds. Then transfer the needed money from your first fund to the new one. Continue this process until you own the portfolio of mutual funds that will best achieve your investment goals.

Continue investing into each fund in your portfolio. Automate the process so that your wealth builds automatically while you go about your life. I worked my way up to five mutual funds and then automated $100 per month into each. Later, I could afford $200 per month into each. Watching the account grow is very satisfying. When prices are down, the money buys more.

When prices are up, the money buys less. But who's ever going to complain about prices going up?

Your mutual fund portfolio may be the only investments you ever own. That's fine. If it's cooking along smoothly and you have no desire to research and choose individual stocks, don't feel bad. It's entirely possible to attain every one of your financial goals with mutual funds alone. Keep investing on a regular basis, watch your portfolio carefully, and enjoy the ride.

Buy Stock in Name-Brand Companies

Once your mutual fund portfolio is established and strong, you might want to invest directly in individual stocks. If so, begin with name-brand companies. They are not very risky, will provide you with pride in ownership, and should perform fairly well.

Also, name-brand companies do not require a lot of research. You already know what they do for a living and you probably have a pretty good idea about their future prospects. For example, you know that Nike shoes are some of the best in the world. They're very popular among U.S. athletes. Then you read in a magazine that Nike is expanding overseas. That sounds promising to you. You check the stock price, see that it's cheap compared to earnings, and decide to buy. Now you can be extra happy watching your daughter win the local track meet. Her future is promising, so is the future of the company whose shoes she's wearing, and so is the future of your shares of stock.

Look for Buying Opportunities

After you've assembled a portfolio of name-brand companies, watch for buying opportunities. Continuing the Nike example, say the stock drops $10 per share after you make your initial purchase. You conclude after reading up on the company that nothing is really wrong. The shoes are still great, the overseas expansion is still on track, and earnings are rising. In short, perhaps this is nothing more than a stock on sale.

So often with name-brand companies, that's exactly what a price decline means. If you have some extra cash, buy more shares of Nike at $10 off. When the stock recovers to your initial buy price, you will have made money. When it keeps rising, you'll make even more.

Discover the Companies of the Future

After establishing a core portfolio of mutual funds, buying stock in name-brand companies and investing more money in your funds regularly and in your stocks when the prices dip, you should consider searching for small companies with huge potential. Notice that you will not venture into this dangerous area of the market until you are sitting atop a strong financial foundation. I don't want to be accused of sending wide-eyed innocents wading into the shark pool. By the time you get to this stage, you should be ready.

The reason that investing in small company stocks can be rewarding is that they can make a lot of money very quickly. They can also lose money quickly, which is why they are the last stage of this progression. I want you to find and buy the next Merck, the next McDonald's, or the next Microsoft. One thousand dollars in the right small company at the right time can buy you a new home. Ten thousand dollars in the right small company at the right time can buy you a new life. It's that potential that makes this last stage such a fine one to consider—when you're ready.

I do want to stress that for every Merck there are a dozen laboratories overrun by rats and filled with dust. For every McDonald's there are hundreds of french fry machines sitting in abandoned restaurants with "condemned" stickers on the cracked windows. For every Microsoft there are thousands of keyboards tossed in dumpsters beside faded profit projection charts. It is not easy to pick winners. It is a breeze to pick losers. Most of us are qualified at birth to do so.

But the potential life-changing investment is out there for you to find. It brings together all of your knowledge and interests. It's growing in the right place at the right time. It's got your name on it. After you build your financial foundation and progress through the layers of safe investments, venture into open waters and find it. Enjoy the journey.

7 | Investing to Retire

Retirement is the most popular investment goal in America. Because retirement is a common goal, there are special ways to invest for it. This chapter will help make sure your retirement plans meet your expectations.

Think About Retirement Now

Now is the time to plan your retirement. I can write that confidently because it's true whether you are twenty years old or fifty years old. Starting early provides you with lots of time to earn money. Starting late is better than not starting at all.

In addition to taking advantage of the years you have available, retirement investing allows you to minimize the taxes you pay and, in some cases, provides you with matching contributions on top of what you save.

Put Time on Your Side

Invested money compounds. Year after year your money earns money, then that total amount earns more money, then that total amount earns even more money, and so on until you own the world. You make earnings on your previous earnings. The more time you have, the more earnings will work for you.

One of my friends began investing $400 every month in her

employer's retirement plan when she was twenty-five years old. Say that her money grows at 10 percent a year until she is sixty-five. She'll retire with $2,529,632.

Another friend began investing $400 every month in his employer's retirement plan when he was thirty-five years old. If his money also grows at 10 percent a year until he's sixty-five, he'll retire with only $904,195.

In fact, if my first friend stopped investing at age thirty-five, she would still retire with more money than my second friend. After her ten years of contributing, she'd have $81,937. Left untouched for thirty years at 10 percent per year, it would be worth $1,625,417.

The lesson in all of this is clear. You should marry somebody who began investing at age twenty-five.

If that's not possible, at least begin your own retirement program right away. If you have less time on your side, try investing greater amounts of money. One advantage about waiting until your later middle years to invest for retirement is that you should make more money than when you were twenty-five. You can compensate for less time with more money.

Minimize Taxes

Retirement plans allow your money to grow tax-deferred or, with the advent of the Roth IRA, tax-free. Here's a bit of advice that will come in handy the rest of your life: Whenever you have a chance to legally postpone taxes, do it.

With nonretirement investments, you need to pay taxes every time you sell at a profit or receive investment income. With retirement investments, you don't pay a penny. All of the profit stays in the account until you retire and begin withdrawing money. At that time, you should be in a lower income tax bracket and the withdrawals are taxed as your income.

The bottom line is that you will save a lot more from within the tax shelter of a retirement account than you will save in a regular taxable account.

Also, many retirement plans allow you to deduct your contributions from your income. That means if you make $40,000 and contribute $2,000 to a traditional individual retirement account, you report that year's income as $38,000.

Benefit from Matching Contributions

Some companies offer retirement plans in which they contribute dollars for you. This benefit is called matching because most companies determine how much they will contribute to your account by looking at how much you contribute. Some companies will contribute $1 for every $1 of yours, others will contribute 50 cents for every $1. The plan varies from company to company.

Also, most companies only match to a certain level, such as 7 percent of your salary. Even though you might be able to save as much as 15 percent or more, the company will match only the first 7 percent. Again, the plans vary.

Needless to say, matching is great. It's the thing I miss most about working for IBM. Now that I'm self-employed, I don't get any retirement dollars from the Big Blue piggy bank. The only money going into my retirement account is the money I put there myself.

If you work for a company that matches your contributions, be sure to at least save the maximum amount that the company will match. You should save the maximum amount you're allowed, period. But if for some reason you don't want to, at least max out the matched dollars. The matching dollars are free money!

Types of Retirement Accounts

There are a bunch of different ways to save for retirement. In many cases, you can take advantage of several at the same time. Retirement accounts are like any other investment accounts, but they bring tax benefits and a few restrictions on when you can get the money. Your retirement accounts hold the same investments you read about in the last chapter: stocks, bonds, the money market, and mutual funds that invest in all three.

Because tax laws change every year, I've purposely kept the details of this section to a minimum. Hopefully the basic idea of each of these accounts will remain in effect when you read this, but the details will probably change a bit. Be sure to check with your brokerage firm or employer about the latest rules.

Individual Retirement Accounts (IRAs)

Anybody can save for their retirement. You don't need to work for a company to plan for your future. As long as you earn income, you qualify.

All of the individual retirement plans in this section are available at any brokerage firm, mutual fund company, or bank. I recommend opening yours at Fidelity or Schwab because they will offer you the widest selection of mutual funds for investing your retirement money. If you ever have questions about any of these plans, call a brokerage firm for a free brochure. You don't need an account with the firm to receive the brochure.

Traditional

The traditional IRA allows you to save up to $2,000 per year tax-deferred. If you don't participate in an employer-sponsored retirement plan, you can deduct the $2,000 from your income and thereby avoid paying taxes on it. If you do participate in an employer plan, you can still contribute to an IRA but may not be able to deduct your contributions from your income. Still, the tax-deferred growth that an IRA provides makes it worthwhile to open one even if you have another retirement plan at work. You just can't have too much money when you retire, can you?

You can't begin withdrawing from your IRA until you're $59^1/_2$ years old. Withdrawing earlier, such as when you are $59^{49}/_{100}$ years old, results in a 10 percent penalty on top of the normal taxes due. There are many exceptions to the penalty, but for the most part, your IRA money needs to stay put until you retire.

Roth

The Roth IRA allows you to save up to $2,000 per year tax-free. Oh yes, I did indeed write tax-free. You are not allowed to deduct the $2,000 from your income, but once it's in the Roth IRA, it can grow to the moon and you will not owe any of it to Uncle Sam. The Roth is so great for investors that many experts predict its quick demise. Surely, they argue, the government will see how much tax revenue it's losing and get rid of the Roth.

I hope not. I opened a Roth within a month of its availability and couldn't be happier. You should probably do the same. You are eligible to contribute the full amount to a Roth IRA if you are single with an adjusted gross income (AGI) of $95,000 or less. The allowable contribution phases out gradually for incomes between $95,001 and $110,000. If you are married, filing jointly, both you and your spouse are eligible to contribute the full amount to a Roth IRA if you have an AGI of $150,000 or less. That's a good deal because your spouse may also contribute up to $2,000 to a separate account—even if he or she has no earned income—as long as your joint compensation at least equals the total amount contributed to the two IRAs (that is, $4,000). If your AGI is higher than $150,000, your ability to contribute to a Roth IRA phases out gradually, then ends for AGIs over $160,000. Different income limits apply to married couples filing separately.

Because you use after-tax dollars to contribute to your Roth IRA, you can withdraw money up to the full amount of your annual contributions at any time without paying taxes or penalties.

Also, you can withdraw up to $10,000 for a first home purchase without paying any federal taxes or penalties. It's quite a deal.

There are a number of details you should know before opening a Roth IRA. Contact any brokerage or bank for complete information.

Simplified Employee Pension (SEP)

The SEP-IRA is as easy to establish as the traditional IRA. SEPs work exactly as traditional IRAs, except that you can contribute up to 13.04 percent of your self-employment income to a maximum of $22,500 per year. You can also deduct the money from your income to save big on taxes.

The best part about SEPs is the huge amount of money they allow you to shelter from taxes. For a lot of people, the measly $2,000 allowed in traditional IRAs is too little.

To qualify for a SEP, you must have self-employment income. However, it does not need to be your only source of income nor does it need to be full time. In other words, if you sell seashells by the seashore on Saturdays, you qualify for a SEP-IRA.

I highly recommend in several places throughout this book that you start some kind of business. The SEP is yet another reason why. Not only does your own business provide you with extra income and lots of tax breaks, it also allows you to sock more of your money away for retirement.

Choosing the Right One

If you have any sort of self-employment income, look strongly at SEP-IRA. It allows you to defer more of your money than any other plan.

If you currently contribute money to a traditional IRA but cannot deduct it from your income, change to a Roth IRA. You can open a Roth IRA and keep your other money in your traditional IRA, or you can convert your traditional to a Roth. If you convert, you will have a Roth conversion IRA and a Roth contributory IRA. Even though you'll have two accounts, you are still limited to contributing a total of $2,000 per year.

A Good Retirement Plan Will Bring You Lots of Fun

The most important thing to remember is that you can open an individual retirement account even if you have a retirement plan through your employer. If you have the extra dough, strongly consider it.

Company Retirement Plans

Most people retire on company plans. The days of pension plans are coming to an end, but investment retirement accounts are shouldering the burden quite well. Some company plans offer matching contributions so that for every dollar amount you contribute, the employer contributes a sum as well.

If you work for a company that offers a retirement plan, request the literature and know what's available to you. Take full advantage of the plan. Here are the most common types of company retirement plans.

401(k)

The 401(k) is the most popular company retirement plan. It allows you to save 20 percent of your salary up to $9,500 per year. Your contributions to a 401(k) happen before taxes, so you do not pay income tax on the money. Then, it grows tax-deferred until you retire.

Most 401(k)s allow you to choose a mixture of mutual funds and the company stock. The drawback is that the choices of funds are usually limited. You won't find nearly the selection that you'll find at Fidelity and Schwab, which is another reason everybody should open an IRA at a brokerage firm. You'll probably find a few index funds, and possibly an actively managed fund for stocks and one for bonds. Look over the list of investments and find the ones that will best achieve your long-term goals.

I discourage you from selecting your employer's stock as part of your retirement investment. You don't want too much of your financial life depending on the success of your employer. You already rely on the company for your income, do you also want to rely on the company for your retirement money? Probably not. If the business hits the skids, you might lose your job and watch the value of your retirement account drop. Skip the company stock. Instead, choose from the other investments offered in the retirement plan.

The best part about a 401(k) plan is not the investments offered, but the plan itself. Nowhere else can you find the benefits of automatic contributions, tax-deductible contributions, tax-deferred growth, and matching.

If your employer offers a 401(k), max it out. That's as plain as I can make it.

403(b)

The 403(b) works the same way as a 401(k), but is offered by nonprofit organizations.

Social Security

Social Security is the government's program to assist you during retirement. It is not intended as your complete retirement plan. Rather, it's supposed to provide you with enough money for shelter, food, and clothing. You must invest wisely to have enough money to enjoy life beyond the basic necessities.

The structure of Social Security is simple. You and your employer pay Social Security taxes into the system during your working years. When you retire, you and your family receive money back from the system.

The amount you receive is determined by how much you earned during your working years and at what age you retire. Benefits increase every year with the Consumer Price Index. In 1997, the cost of living adjustment was 2.9 percent.

The table below shows the Social Security Administration's estimate of what percentage of your annual income would be replaced by Social Security. The table assumes that you begin receiving benefits at age sixty-five, and that your nonworking spouse receives a spousal benefit.

Social Security Annual Income Replacement		
Final Salary	Single	Married
$20,000	48%	72%
$50,000	31%	46%
$100,000	16%	24%

Most financial planners recommend that your retirement income equal around 80 percent of your pretax wages during your final working years. As you can see from the above table, Social Security will provide far less than 80 percent for all but the lowest wage earners.

You can get a free estimate of your future benefits by calling Social Security at 800-772-1213 and requesting form SSA-7004, "Request for Earnings and Benefit Estimate Statement." If you are fifty-eight or older, the statement is automatically mailed to your home address each year.

While you can't rely on Social Security for all of your retirement income, it's nice to know that some of the burden will be lifted from your shoulders. I recommend that you consider Social Security icing on the cake. Pretend it doesn't exist. Then assemble your own investment program that will provide for the retirement lifestyle you desire.

That way, your Social Security benefits will only add to the good times. As I mentioned earlier, you can't have too much money in retirement.

How Much to Invest for Retirement

You should max out every retirement account option available to you. If your employer allows you to set aside 15 percent of your paycheck to a 401(k) plan, then set aside the full 15 percent. Because you will not be able to deduct contributions to a traditional IRA, open a Roth IRA and contribute the annual maximum of $2,000. That breaks into monthly payments of $166.66. If you earn any self-employed income, open a SEP-IRA and contribute what you can.

Only when reaching the SEP-IRA stage should you consider taming your retirement investments. The SEP allows you to set aside up to $22,500 per year. If you are young and have already maxed out your 401(k) and opened a Roth IRA, then you can consider forgetting the SEP-IRA altogether or contributing just a small amount.

The reason you should invest as much as possible in retirement accounts is that the money enjoys such great tax advantages. Packing your retirement accounts to the gills between age twenty-five and thirty-five will set you up for life. If you can continue investing in them beyond age thirty-five, you'll live the life of Riley.

But be nice to yourself and your family. I'm not saying you need to skip vacations and holidays and cut down on grocery costs by teaching your children how to graze. What I am saying is that as you get smarter about your spending habits and free up more of your income for investing, take care of your retirement options first. Only after you have fully funded them should you turn your attention to nonretirement investments.

If you would like to map out exactly how much you need to save for retirement, call Fidelity (800-544-8888) and Schwab (800-435-4000) for free retirement planning booklets. They include worksheets that factor your income, retirement plans, and Social Security benefits to determine the amount of money you need to save each month toward retirement.

8 | All About Insurance

An important part of your personal financial plan is protecting what you have. There's little point spending less than you earn and investing the difference if you allow years of hard work to be wiped out by a single accident. That's why you carry insurance.

The Right Way to Handle Insurance

Too many people get confused by insurance because there are so many options. Knowing the very simple reason you carry insurance will help cut through the clutter. So here it is:

You buy insurance to protect your money.

That's it. You spend a small amount of money on insurance to prevent spending a big amount on catastrophes. Because the only purpose of insurance is to protect your money, it makes sense to spend as little of your money as possible when buying insurance.

As simple as the purpose of insurance is, sales representatives and advertisements will do their best to confuse you. You'll be told that health insurance is there to protect your health. No, it isn't. Only your lifestyle choices and a pinch of good genetics can do that. Health insurance just limits the amount of your money you need to spend when you become unhealthy.

You'll be told that auto insurance protects your car and the other car in an accident. No it doesn't. By the time you need to use your insurance, the cars are already wrecked. Only your good driving habits and the good habits of those joining you on the road can protect your car. Automobile insurance just limits the amount of your money you need to spend repairing cars when you wreck.

Insurance Only Defends Your Money

Life insurance adds a twist to the purpose of insurance. Instead of protecting your money, it provides your loved ones with extra money when you die. In other words, it's just another form of investment. You should still spend as little as possible to get as much as possible in return.

Premiums and Deductibles

The two most important terms for you to know about insurance are *premium* and *deductible*.

The premium is the charge you pay for the insurance coverage and can vary widely from company to company for the same amount of coverage. Think of the premium as the insurance policy's price tag. Just as you'll want to shop around for the best price on a car repair, so you'll want to shop around for the best premium on your insurance policies. In Los Angeles, I have found annual liability insurance premiums on my RX-7 that range from $2,400 per year down to $600. Both policies covered the same amount of damage.

The deductible is the fixed dollar amount you must pay before the insurance begins paying. For example, say your auto insurance policy carries a $500 deductible. If you broadside your neighbor's new Cadillac, you'll need to pay $500 out of your pocket before your insurance starts paying for the repairs.

The relationship between an insurance policy's premium and deductible is like the two ends of a see-saw. As the deductible rises, the premium falls. As the deductible falls, the premium rises. Because you pay the premium whether you have an accident or not, it makes sense to lower its price as much as possible. That means a higher deductible, which is a sum that you will only need to pay in case of an accident.

As you can see, one of the easiest ways to cut your insurance costs is to accept the highest deductible you can afford. A lot of people think that they're saving money by paying as little a deductible as possible. So they fork out higher insurance payments every month—the sum of which can far outweigh the deductible savings—to save on the amount they will pay *if* they ever need to use the insurance.

Dumb, dumb, dumb. Think for a second about how the insurance industry makes money. It takes your payments and hopes to high heaven that you never need to file a claim. When you file a claim, the insurance company must then pay money to satisfy the claim. They need to fix your car, fix your home, pay for your hospital bills, and so on.

Don't Give Your Money to Insurance Fat Cats

If every insurance policy ever written resulted in claims, there'd be no insurance industry. It could not profit unless it charged so much for the insurance that people would simply start using their own money to cover themselves in emergencies. Do you follow this? The fact that there is an insurance industry means that the odds of you ever needing to file a claim are fairly low. Therefore, the odds of you ever needing to pay a deductible are fairly low.

Compare that to the odds of your having to pay the premium. It's guaranteed. You'll pay it every month or quarter or year, depending on the policy, whether you file a claim or not.

In case you don't believe me, I'm bringing in a reinforcement. In his book *The Only Investment Guide You'll Ever Need*, Andrew Tobias explored the homeowner's insurance policy available on a $500,000 home in West Hollywood. An insurance company charged a premium of $2,803 a year with a $100 deductible; $2,503 a year with a $250 deductible; $2,228 a year with a $500 deductible; and $1,802 a year with a $1,000 deductible. Looking over the numbers, Tobias asks, "Where is the madman who would pay an extra $1,001 a year ($2,803 versus $1,802) to get an extra $900 of coverage ($100 versus $1,000 deductible)?"

Be smart and ratchet your deductibles to the highest available level that you can afford. Save on your regular premium payments with the knowledge that you will probably never need to pay the higher deductible payment. Even if you do need to pay, the money you saved on premiums can be invested and grown to more than enough to cover the deductible. With all of the wise money management tips you've gleaned from this book, you should have plenty of assets to cover the highest deductible available on all of your insurance policies.

Don't Waste Money on Small Items

Because insurance is supposed to protect your money, don't buy insurance where no protection is needed. You may laugh at the self-evidence of that advice, but take a look around at how many people are doing just that.

People buy credit unemployment protection on their Visa or Mastercard. Why? To protect them in case they can't make the minimum monthly payments. So they pay an insurance company just in case they can't pay their credit card company.

People buy extended warranties on merchandise that rarely breaks. When your VCR breaks, you buy a new one. Even if you do repair it, the cost of the repair is probably less than the cost of a warranty.

If you own something that is not expensive to repair, don't insure it. Never buy insurance for any expense that would not devastate you. Never buy insurance to guard against expenses that will probably never happen. That means you should skip all warranties as I just discussed, pass by flight insurance kiosks at the airport, and turn your nose up at rental insurance.

Get as Much Coverage as Possible

When you do buy insurance, be sure that it covers a lot for your money. Get health insurance that covers you in case of an auto accident. Get life insurance that covers you in case of a plane crash. Consider an umbrella policy that covers everything.

If one affordable policy can take care of a bunch of little items, you won't be tempted to buy a separate policy on every one of life's risks. As if flying on a commercial airline is that risky. You'd be smarter buying banana-peel-on-the-grocery-store-floor insurance.

Insuring What You Own

The things you own can be expensive to repair after a catastrophe. That is, the things that you should bother insuring. Remember, don't insure the little stuff that isn't expensive to repair. Don't be a madman.

Automobile Insurance

Your car is coming up as, yet again, a cause of great expense. Just as you will save on the purchase price of your car by buying used, you will also save on your insurance by buying used.

The first reason you'll save is that a used car has a lower value than a new car and will therefore be cheaper to repair. So insurance companies will charge less for a policy covering repairs on your car.

The second reason you'll save is that if your car's value is low enough, you can opt out of its coverage altogether. You'll still need to carry insurance on the other guy's car, but not on your own. That's what I've chosen to do. My RX-7 is worth around $4,000. Because the odds of ever crashing are so low, I've chosen to shoulder the entire burden of repairing it myself. I carry the legally required insurance to cover the costs of repairing the other guy's car, but that's it. Going this route saves me around $1,000 every year on insurance. At that savings, it doesn't take long to have enough money to more than cover the cost of repairs, *if* they ever happen.

The Four Types of Coverage

There are four types of auto coverage. They are liability, medical, collision, and comprehensive:

- Liability insurance covers the other person's car and medical if you cause an accident. This coverage is required in most states because it's unfair to hit some-body's car and then stick them with a bill to repair it. If it's your fault, you should pay. To make sure that you can, you need to carry liability insurance. As I just mentioned, lia-bility is the only coverage I carry.

- Medical insurance covers your hospital bills and the hospital bills of any passengers in your vehicle. However, if you take my earlier advice about buying the broadest coverage possible, your health insurance will already cover you in case of an auto accident. It will do so for far less than your auto insurance, and you should have health insurance anyway. So don't spend twice for the same coverage.

- Collision insurance covers damages to your car caused in an accident. It is always optional because the only person you could possibly harm by not carrying collision is your-self. And who cares about you anyway? Only people with expensive cars should carry collision insurance. People who drive used cars can—heh, heh—skip collision insur-ance entirely.

- Comprehensive insurance covers all damages to your car caused by something other than an accident, such as fire, flood, earthquake, tornado, theft, hurricane, vandalism, and so on. You buy it in addition to the other auto insur-ance you carry. Once again, owning an inexpensive car pays off because there's little at risk by not carrying com-prehensive insurance.

How to Save on Auto Insurance

Again, the best way to cut your auto insurance bill is to drive a cheaper car. The next best way is to accept as high a deductible as you can afford.

After that, shop around extensively. It's worth an afternoon on the phone asking and answering questions to find the cheapest policy. I recommend starting with Amica (800-992-6422) because it's the most affordable auto insurance company I've found. Amica does not advertise. It gets most of its business through referrals. When you call, tell the representative that you read about Amica in this book. That way I'll get 10 percent of your premium payments. Just kidding.

After calling Amica, call Colonial Penn (800-847-1729) and Geico (800-841-3000). If you are an active-duty or retired military officer, or a dependent of one, also try USAA (800-531-8080). If you live in California, also try 20th Century (800-211-7233). Get quotes from each, then compare them with quotes from local insurance companies in your phone book.

Drive safely. Most insurance companies will lower the premium for people with no accidents or traffic tickets. Be sure to tell every company you call about your clean driving record. If you don't have a clean record, keep quiet. They'll probably ask anyway, but don't go out of your way to tell them about the time you made it across town in seven minutes by screaming through every yellow light.

Drive a safe car. Most insurance companies will lower the premium on cars equipped with safety features like airbags, anti-lock brakes, and car alarms.

Ask about a household discount. If your household insures more than one car, you'll probably get a break by insuring all of them with the same company. Be sure to ask.

Homeowner's or Renter's Insurance

When you buy a home, most mortgage lenders require that you carry homeowner's insurance. It's not a bad idea, anyway. Replacing your home and everything in it would be awfully expensive. Homeowner's insurance will cover against property damage and also against lawsuits. You never know when a neighbor will trip over a crack in your driveway and yell, "Jackpot!"

If you rent, consider renter's insurance. It will protect you from property loss in case of natural disaster, theft, and such. It will also protect you from lawsuits.

Three Components

There are three components in a homeowner's policy. They are dwelling coverage, personal property coverage, and liability coverage. Dwelling coverage does not apply to renters.

Dwelling Coverage

Dwelling coverage is the part of your homeowner's policy that pays to rebuild your home. Renters do not carry dwelling coverage because they do not own the property. If their building crumbles to the ground, renters gather up their belongings and walk to the apartment building across the street. The property owner must shoulder the cost of rebuilding.

The amount of dwelling coverage you carry should be based on what it would cost to completely rebuild your home. Notice that this amount has nothing to do with the value of your mortgage or the purchase price of your home.

Be careful that your insurance policy includes *guaranteed replacement cost.* That means that if your home crumbles and rebuilding it ends up costing more than the amount of your coverage, the insurance company will still pay for it. They'll eat the difference.

Personal Property Coverage

Personal property coverage protects against the loss of everything on your property besides your home, such as your television, computer system, stereo, and furniture. The amount of personal property coverage you carry is usually valued at 50 to 75 percent of your dwelling coverage. So if you carry $100,000 in dwelling coverage, you're probably covered for at least $50,000 in personal property damages.

Be sure that your personal property coverage insures for the *replacement cost* of your property, not the *actual cash value.* Actual cash value would mean that if your ten-year-old VCR was stolen, you'd only get the $5 or so that it's worth. Replacement cost would mean that you'd get the price of a brand-new VCR.

To be thoroughly covered by your personal property insurance, you should inventory your belongings. Take photos of the big stuff, keep receipts, and list the purchase date and price of items without receipts. Make a copy of your inventory and store it in a safe place.

Liability Coverage

Liability coverage protects your money from lawsuits filed by someone injured on your property. Carry enough insurance to cover one to two times the value of your financial assets. If you carry enough liability insurance, you can start tossing marbles on your doorstep just to see if anybody sues.

How to Save on Homeowner's Insurance

Remember to sign up for the highest deductible you can afford. That's the first step and the one that will probably save you the most money.

Next, shop around just as you did with auto insurance. In fact, call the same companies I listed on pages 185–86. Also call local agents for State Farm, Allstate, and others in your phone book. Do not assume that the company giving you the cheapest auto insurance will give you the cheapest homeowner's insurance. Rates depend on a lot of criteria.

Ask for a list of available discounts. Some policies will be cheaper if your home has a strong security system, fire alarms, smoke detectors, rounded corners, and padded walls. You never know what might save money.

Ask if you can save money by combining your auto and home insurance with the same company. If so, be sure to compare it to the total amount you would be paying with the best total amount you could get by carrying policies from different companies. It's worth the hassle of writing an extra check each month if it saves you hundreds per year.

Umbrella Insurance

An umbrella insurance policy can be a wise move if you have a lot of assets to protect. It goes beyond the coverage offered by your homeowner's and auto policies to extend coverage to values beyond $1 million. It's fairly cheap, too. A $1 million policy costs around $250 per year. If you've got a million bucks to protect, you won't miss the $250.

How does it work? Just like the name implies, umbrella insurance is an additional policy that arches over and above your other insurance policies. If you exceed the limits of your homeowner's insurance, a $1 million umbrella policy would kick in to cover the difference. If you wreck your car into a trailer full of military satellite equipment, your umbrella policy will help pay the damages beyond your auto insurance.

Finally, umbrella insurance covers lawsuits unrelated to your home or car. If you get sued for anything and need to pay, your umbrella policy will pay the cost up to the limit of your coverage.

Contact your auto or homeowner's insurance company for umbrella information.

Insuring Yourself and Your Family

Nothing is as precious as your life and the lives of your family. The real damage of a car accident is not the car, it's the people. The real catastrophe of a home crumbling has a lot more to do with the bodies inside than with the bricks and lumber.

This section presents information on health, disability, and life insurance.

Health Insurance

The best health insurance is to stay healthy. Don't smoke. Exercise three times a week. Eat fruits and vegetables. Drink lots of water. Relax.

After that, there's the paid kind of health insurance. If you're lucky, you can get it through your employer. You'll probably need to pick up some of the cost yourself, but it will be cheaper and easier than finding coverage on your own.

If you are self-employed, unemployed, or employed by a company that does not provide health insurance, it's time for another round of comparison shopping.

Fee-for-Service and Managed Care

There are two types of health insurance: *fee-for-service* and *managed care*.

Fee-for-service allows you to choose your doctor, find a new one at any time, and seek specialists as needed. This privilege is expensive, however. You not only pay an annual premium, you also pay a deductible that ranges from hundreds to thousands of dollars per year. Beyond the deductible, the insurance company usually pays 80 percent of the medical costs. That means you pay the remaining 20 percent. With today's medical bills, even the 20 percent can be a huge burden. In one week, my neighbor ran up $20,000 in a nationally known Los Angeles hospital. Meeting his $1,500 deductible and paying 20 percent of the remaining bill cost him a grand total of $5,200.

Managed care costs less but also provides less. Participants receive a list of member doctors to choose from. Using a doctor outside the plan is either not allowed or costs a lot. Most managed care plans charge a monthly premium and then a modest co-payment for each office visit. The two most common managed care programs are *health maintenance organizations* (*HMOs*) and *preferred provider organizations* (*PPOs*).

HMOs are the most restrictive of the two. In an HMO, you'll need your primary physician's permission to seek the advice of a specialist who must also participate in the HMO. In a PPO, you are usually free to see a specialist whenever you'd like. That's really the only difference between an HMO and a PPO.

HMOs Provide Excellent Health Care Until You Get Sick

HMOs have horrible reputations for providing the worst health care in history. They are corporations, not caring organizations. They run patients through the system in herd formation, lose medical records, and do not value personal relationships. The doctor you see today will be gone tomorrow. You are a body, nothing more. HMOs have earned a dubious motto on the streets of Los Angeles. People say, "HMOs: providing excellent health care until you get sick." Many are so bad that new patients must sign a form agreeing to a set of rules for suing the company. That's generally a bad sign.

PPOs seem to be the better form of managed care. They are still relatively affordable, but allow you to build a personal rapport with your doctor. You become a real person with feelings, not a line on the corporate balance sheet.

If you can afford a fee-for-service plan, do it. You may get special rates if you insure your entire family. It might even become as affordable as a managed care program.

If you cannot afford fee-for-service, try to find a PPO. If you can't find one, research every HMO in your area. Talk to people who have been seriously ill and received care through one of the HMOs. Learn from their experience. Go with the best HMO you can find.

Getting the Best Value on Health Insurance

Here are some guidelines to help you find the best health insurance value:

- If you are getting health insurance only as a precaution, then get the highest deductible you can afford. If you expect to be using your health insurance regularly, then determine the right balance between your deductible and premium payments. Only you know your situation, so only you can see the best tradeoff.
- Consider your special needs. While many people keep health insurance only for matters of serious emergency, others have ongoing health trouble that requires regular visits and lots of medications. The bare bones plan for the first type of person probably wouldn't fit the needs of the second type of person. When shopping for insurance, be sure to compare the costs of coverage you will actually use.
- Try finding a group plan. If you are part of an organization that offers group health coverage, check into it. Anything purchased in bulk is cheaper per unit. Try to be one of the units getting in cheaply. Start with your professional memberships, religious affiliations, civic groups, and so on.
- Get the most for your money. Does your health insurance cover dental? Vision? Chiropractic care? If not, find out how much the additional coverage will cost.
- Know the policy on prescriptions. Some plans offer any prescription for only $5, others pick up a portion of each medicine's cost.
- Save money on prescriptions that you must buy. Obviously,

if your plan charges $5 for any prescription then there's no point shopping around. But if you're paying the tab, be a smart shopper. Buy generic when you can. Call several pharmacies in your area. If you can wait, consider ordering medicines through the mail. Try Diversified Prescription Deliver (800-452-1976) and Medi-Mail (800-922-3444).

- Don't settle for a lifetime cap that's less than $1 million. Some insurance plans limit their payments to a maximum amount over your lifetime. Anything less than $1 million won't be enough.

- Make sure your policy is guaranteed renewable. If it is, then the company can't stop covering you or raise your premiums when you file a claim.

Consider Outpatient Clinics

Something that I've tried recently was skipping the traditional plans altogether and going straight to an outpatient clinic. All I had was a simple pain in my side for several days—it turned out to be an alien.

Getting the pain checked through my main health insurance would have left me entirely within the cost of the deductible. In other words, I would shoulder 100 percent of the cost. It was near the end of the year, so I knew that I wouldn't have time to exceed the deductible and start charging expenses to insurance.

A friend told me about an outpatient clinic that charges only $59 for any visit. That was cheaper than visiting a doctor and my pain seemed like a simple enough problem to diagnose. So I gave it a try.

It turned out to be a great choice. I walked in, signed a sheet, paid with my credit card, and was called to the examination room in less than a minute. A nurse prechecked me. Moments later, a friendly doctor gave me a thorough examination and discovered the alien. He recommended a few over-the-counter drugs and told me I'd be fine.

I saved a lot of money by going to the outpatient clinic. You should consider finding a good one in your area.

Disability Insurance

Your most valuable asset is your ability to earn income. It pays for your home, car, health, food, and everything else. Losing your ability to earn income can be disastrous. The emergency reserve money that you will maintain after reading this book will save you for a while, but eventually it will run out.

Disability insurance will protect your income if you become disabled.

How Much for How Long

You should get a policy that provides you with at least 70 percent of your income. If you use this book to create a solid financial foundation with years' worth of money invested, then consider a disability policy that covers less of your income. If you have few bills and a lot of money invested, you might decide to skip disability altogether.

To decide, ask yourself what would happen to your family if you could not work for twelve months. If you would lose your home and car, get dragged to debtor's court by your credit card companies, and have no money for food, get a disability policy that will cover enough of your income to save the day. If you would just lie in bed writing checks without consequence, then plan a skimpier disability policy.

Once you've decided on an amount, you'll need to choose how long you will receive income. When you become disabled, most policies won't begin paying you until three to six months have passed. That's called the *elimination period*. Once the elimination period is over, you stop paying premiums and the policy begins to pay you. The amount of time that you receive payments is called the *benefits period*. You can adjust both periods.

To be completely safe, get a benefits period that takes you to the age of retirement. If the worst happens, you might be disabled for the rest of your working life. It would be quite a shock to suddenly have your disability income stopped short when you are ten years from retirement. To avoid that, get a policy with a benefit period that takes you through the rest of your working years.

Employer Plans

Most corporations provide their employees with disability insurance. It's not the same as worker's compensation, by the way. Worker's compensation protects you in case of injury sustained on the job. Disability insurance protects you in case of injuries sustained anywhere at any time.

Employer plans usually cover around 60 percent of your income to a maximum monthly payment amount. Sometimes, employees are given a choice between disability insurance and life insurance. If you are single with no dependents, take the disability.

Check with your employer for details on its disability insurance plan.

Individual Plans

If you're self-employed, you'll need to shop around for the best disability coverage. There are several features you should look for.

Understand whether the policy covers your *own occupation* or *any occupation*. An own occupation policy will pay benefits if you cannot do the job you normally do. An any occupation policy will pay only if you cannot do any job. Naturally, own occupation policies are preferable because a highly paid employee would be reluctant to take a low-paying job. Because they are more appealing, own occupation policies are more expensive. You should choose one only if you are in a specialized high-income job. Some policies offer a hybrid of the two types of coverage. The first two years are own occupation, followed by any occupation for the remainder of the benefit period.

Be sure that your policy covers both sickness and accidents. The last thing you want is to come down with yellow fever only to discover that your policy does not cover sickness.

Your policy should be both *noncancelable* and *guaranteed renewable*. Noncancelable means that your insurance company can't stop your policy because you do indeed get sick or injured. Believe it or not, policies exist that can stop at just the time you need them. Guaranteed renewable means that you can renew your policy every year without undergoing a medical checkup. It also keeps your insurance company from raising your premiums due to the volume of claims you've filed.

Residual benefits are a nice feature on some plans. This option means that if you are disabled in such a way that you will need to work only part-time for the remainder of your career, you will receive partial benefits. The insurance payment will make up the difference between what you earn part-time and what you would earn if you worked full-time.

Finally, get a *cost-of-living adjustment (COLA)* option. Having a COLA on your policy means that your payments will increase over time to reflect the rising price of goods and services. It won't do you much good to receive 1999 wages when you become disabled in 2010. A COLA will guarantee that you receive appropriate wages for the time. Look for a COLA of 3 to 4 percent a year.

How to Save on Disability Insurance

The elimination period of your disability insurance is similar to the deductible on any other insurance policy. The higher the deductible, the lower the premium. With disability insurance, the longer your elimination period, the lower your premium. That means, of course, that you would need to be able to survive without benefits during the entire elimination period. If you manage your money wisely and have an adequate emergency reserve with other investments to help, you should have no trouble surviving a long elimination period.

After that basic step, the shopping begins. Start with Termquote (800-444-8376) and Wholesale Insurance Network (800-808-5810). They will search among several policies from different companies to find the most affordable one for you. Compare the quotes you receive with quotes from local brokers in your phone book.

Ask the various companies you call if they offer gradual-payment plans. These allow you to pay lower premiums when you're young and higher ones as you age. Be sure to look carefully at the plan you're offered. Sometimes the gradual-payments end up costing far more in the end. Don't let rearranged numbers fool you. Add them up, then go with the best bargain.

Life Insurance

This is the biggie. More people are ripped off every year on life insurance than probably any other financial product. There are a lot of emotions involved and sales people use them to their full power. Let's make sure you know what you need and only what you need.

When you die, your dependents lose your earnings and become responsible for all of the household payments and all of your debts. The situation could leave your dependents in a financial nightmare at a time when they are emotionally devastated. The last thing you want your family having to face right after your death is a house full of unpaid bills and no money to pay them.

That's where life insurance fits in. Life insurance provides your family with money when you die. It's a financial safety net to take care of them during their time of grief and, hopefully, through many years beyond.

When you die, your life insurance policy pays a lump sum called a *death benefit*. Beneficiaries are not taxed on the death benefit when they receive it. Your survivors use the money to pay immediate expenses like your funeral and household bills. Hopefully, the death benefit gets invested to provide years of ongoing financial support.

Now, you can see that life insurance has nothing to do with your life except that it cashes in when you cash out. It exists to save your dependents, which leads to the most important lesson about life insurance:

If you don't have any dependents, you don't need life insurance.

If you are single and the only person who depends on you is you, then you've read all you need to read about life insurance. Congratulations. You just saved a bundle. Insurance reps will try to convince you that you still need to insure. One of their favorite tactics is guilt. They will say that your family will need to pick up the tab on your debts. Baloney. Unless they've co-signed a loan, they aren't responsible. Your debts die when you die. Creditors will take what they can from your assets or they'll simply write off the loss.

The second life insurance lesson is that if your spouse works and earns enough money to support the household, then you still don't need life insurance. The simplest way to decide whether you need life insurance is to look at the people in your life and decide if they will be financially affected by your death. If not, you don't need life insurance. If so, you do.

Term Life Insurance

This is the type you need, if you need any life insurance at all. Term insurance protects you for a specified period of time, called the term. When the term expires, you can renew for another term. You buy only what you need, when you need it, for how long you need it.

When you're young, you pay very little for term life insurance because there's only a small chance that you will die soon. For a death benefit of $100,000, a thirty-year-old nonsmoker would pay around $250 per year. The premium increases each time you renew because you are older and there's a greater chance that you will die during the term of the insurance.

No agent will recommend term insurance to you. The commissions are low, so you'll never know. But now you do and I'll discuss ways to find the best term life insurance bargains in a moment. But first you need to know about the bad kind of life insurance.

Permanent Life Insurance

Permanent life insurance is one of the stupidest financial products I've ever encountered. It's a life insurance plan with a death benefit like term insurance, but it also has a silly feature called *cash value*. That's why permanent life insurance is also called cash value life insurance. The cash value feature allows you to save part of your insurance premiums in an investment account that grows tax-deferred.

"Why," you wonder, "would I buy a life insurance policy to save money?" Because if you hadn't read this book you might have been talked into it by somebody who makes a big commission off your ignorance. Cash value policies pay the highest commissions. In fact, the average commission paid on cash value life insurance is eight times the commission paid on a comparable term life policy. Therefore, cash value policies are the products that sales reps push the hardest. Unfortunately, cash value policies make sense for the least number of people. The majority of cash value insurance policyholders would be better off with term insurance.

It Doesn't Make Sense

The representatives will try to sell you on permanent life insurance by saying that you won't be able to afford the high term insurance payments when you're old. But guess what? You probably won't need any life insurance when you're old because your children will be grown and you and your spouse will be living off your retirement benefits anyway. Nobody needs a death benefit.

They'll tell you it's convenient to borrow against your policy. That's a good one. It's your money! Since when does it make sense to pay somebody for a boatload of insurance just so you can have convenient access to your money? You don't pay for access to your checking account. You shouldn't pay for access to any of your money.

They'll say the tax-deferred status of the cash portion of your policy is smart planning. It's true that tax-deferral is nice to have, but you can have it for free in a retirement account that you set up with Fidelity or Schwab. You do not need life insurance to benefit from tax-deferred savings.

The most common forms of permanent life insurance are *whole life, universal life,* and *variable life*. Whole and universal policies invest your cash value portion in bonds. Because you'll carry your life insurance for a long period of time, this strategy almost guarantees that your cash will underperform the stock investments you could have purchased on your own. Variable policies provide you with a menu of mutual funds to choose from. The funds are not as good as the ones you can get outside of the life insurance policy.

So, do permanent life insurance policies ever make sense? Only if you are looking for ways to shield some of your estate from taxes after you die. Even then, there are a lot of choices that might be better than permanent life insurance.

The bottom line for the purpose of this book is that you do not want to buy a permanent or cash value life insurance policy.

How to Save on Term Life Insurance

Start by calling Quotesmith (800-431-1147), SelectQuote (800-343-1985), Termquote (800-444-8376), and Wholesale Insurance Network (800-808-5810). They will provide you with a list of term policies and prices from which to choose.

Term insurance offers the ability to adjust how often your premium increases. It can happen every year, every five years, ten years, and so on. The more often it increases, the lower your initial premium payments will be. If you lock in the payments for fifteen years, the insurance company will increase the premium to compensate for the increased risk of your death. Ask for quotes at different levels of frequency so you can find the best balance for you.

Buy only the death benefit you need. It's tempting to sign up for a multimillion-dollar death benefit. It will cost a lot more than a modest death benefit. Most guides I've read recommend that you get a death benefit equal to at least eight years of your after-tax annual salary. That's a ballpark figure. A better way to estimate is to figure how many years of your income you want to replace. Then, multiply that number by 80 percent. For example, if you want to replace ten years of income, you should carry a death benefit worth at least eight years of your after-tax annual salary.

Finally, stop your policy when you no longer have dependents. When your children are grown and you have built enough of a financial foundation to support your spouse after you die, cancel your term life insurance. Nobody needs it anymore. Use the money you were spending on premiums and take a cruise around the world.

9 | Taxes, Toddlers, and Tools

To round out your financial happiness, this chapter shows quick ways to cut your tax bill, discusses the importance of teaching your children about money, and provides a list of resources to help you manage your finances.

Cut Your Taxes

Taxes will probably be the biggest expense of your life. Every time you earn a buck, you owe tax. That means it's a frequent expense. As you learned earlier in the book, repeating expenses need to be examined carefully for ways to cut back. The savings will be tremendous.

This chapter barely pokes a finger into the tax code ocean. But it covers a few big things that can help you out. Getting a few big financial decisions right is better than getting a whole slew of little ones right.

Don't Get a Refund

If you receive a tax refund every year, then you are paying too much tax. You don't want to lend the government your money for a whole year. You want to pay only what you owe. You should keep the rest of your money invested at a competitive rate of return. The investment growth on the money that you've been getting refunded every year could be a lot.

The Beardstown Ladies offer a nice example on this point in their *Guide to Smart Spending for Big Savings*. Say you receive $2,500 a year in tax refunds. If you had $2,000 less withheld from your paycheck and invested the difference in an investment that yields 8 percent a year, in twenty years you'd have $9,853. If you did it every year for twenty years, you'd end up with $108,019. All by keeping your money invested for you instead of giving Uncle Sam an interest-free loan.

That example shows one of the easiest ways for employees to save on taxes. Just increase your number of exemptions. There's no law against setting them at any level. The forms guide you to a recommended number of exemptions based on your dependents and other factors. But you can skip the recommendations and enter any number of exemptions you want. If you're getting a refund every year, increase your number of paycheck exemptions to decrease the taxes you pay. Then, invest the extra money immediately for maximum return.

If you are self-employed, send less money in. Find the areas where you are overpaying, then stop doing it! Don't be nervous and think that the IRS is going to penalize you. If you are receiving a refund, you are paying too much tax. Pay less to get to the amount you're supposed to pay.

Start a Business

Even if you are employed full time, start a business on the side. Not only can you make extra money doing something that you enjoy, you can also save a lot of money on your taxes.

Tax laws were written for people in business. As an employee, you can't deduct much of anything from your income. As a business person, you can deduct almost everything.

Buying a new computer? If you use it for business, you can deduct the cost from your income. Driving across town for supplies? As long as they're used in your business, you can deduct the mileage from your income. Nearly any expense you incur in the process of conducting business is deductible.

If you're really clever, you can find ways to make your normal expenses a part of your business expenses. For instance, say you are driving across town to an office supply store that

Start a Business for Tax Benefits

happens to be next to a grocery store. Because you drove to the office supply store, the drive mileage was a business expense along with the price of the paper and envelopes you bought. However, as long as you're parked in the shopping center, you can stop into the grocery store for milk and eggs. You can now write off the auto mileage for a drive that you would have had to take anyway.

A great deduction is the home office deduction. It allows you to write off a portion of your housing expense—whether it's a mortgage payment or rent—because you use part of your home for business. Although claiming a home office deduction increases the chances of being audited, you should still do it. There's nothing illegal about claiming a home office if you really use one. You may want to double-check an annual tax guide to make sure that your usage of your home is a legitimate business use.

Keep all of your receipts in a folder labeled with the tax year or, if you're an especially organized person, keep receipts in folders labeled with tax categories. For instance, your computer receipt would go into office equipment. Your meal receipts would go into business meals.

One very easy way to track all of your business expenses and make tax time simple is to use personal finance software. Both Intuit *Quicken* and Microsoft *Money* allow you to create spending categories that are automatically assigned to specific lines on your tax form. At the end of the year, you simply create a tax report and know immediately what to enter on each line of your return. By filing the receipts as you enter them into the software, you also have the proof you'll need if you are ever audited. This is the system I use and I find it to be about as painless as tax management can be.

Your business should make money. If you lose money on your business for too long, the IRS considers it a hobby and will no longer allow you to make deductions. But being profitable should be your goal anyway.

So, start a profitable business and start writing off your expenses.

Contribute More to Retirement

Remember that contributions to many retirement plans are tax-deductible. Max out your contributions to company retirement plans. Doing so will reduce your taxable income and prepare you for a wealthy retirement.

Open an IRA. The Roth IRA won't allow you to deduct your contributions, but it will grow tax-free forever. That's still a form of tax savings.

The traditional IRA can be deducted from your income every year if you qualify. Most people should choose the Roth over the traditional IRA, but be sure to read the retirement literature carefully to see what's best for you. If you qualify, a traditional IRA can shave $2,000 a year from your reported income.

If you are self-employed, don't forget to look at the SEP-IRA. It allows you to set aside up to 13.04 percent of your annual income tax-deferred. That can save you a lot on taxes.

To read more about retirement plans, turn back to chapter 7.

Stop Worrying About Audits

First of all, audits only happen to about 1 percent of the tax filers every year. Your odds of ever being audited are very low.

More important, an audit is nothing to fear as long as you're honest in your tax returns. There is nothing wrong with minimizing your taxes in legitimate ways. Tax reduction strategies are based on tax law. Deducting business expenses and contributing toward your own retirement are not crimes. They are smart activities that the IRS does not tax. You will not get in trouble for minimizing your taxes in legal ways.

Of the people who get audited, 20 percent owe nothing after the audit and 5 percent get money from the IRS. Thus, only 75 percent of the 1 percent of people who are audited end up owing money after the audit.

Teach Your Toddlers About Money

You've read about my family on a few pages in this book. I mentioned that my grandfather taught me how to save, that my father showed me the evils of debt, and that my mother demonstrated the art of bargain shopping. I was a lucky kid. Not everybody benefits from sound financial lessons early in life.

Make sure your kids are among the best-educated money managers on the planet. Show them why debt is bad, show them how to save, show them the joy of owning property instead of buying on credit, and show them that small amounts of money invested today will turn into big amounts tomorrow.

Your children should graduate from high school knowing that they are already wealthy because of the time on their side. Every eighteen-year-old is a millionaire waiting to happen. If they spend less than they earn and invest the difference, they will never suffer financial misery.

A great way to help a child understand money is to open a mutual fund account for him or her. Then, offer matching contributions. Every time your child contributes $1, you contribute $1. When your child gets a high-paying job at the local pizza parlor and begins contributing hundreds each month, you may have to amend your policy. Contribute $1 for each of the child's first $100, then 50¢ on each of the next $100, then 10¢ on subsequent dollars.

Teach Good Financial Habits to Your Children

If your child starts contributing a lot of money to the account, stop teaching about investing and start teaching about taxes. Take 30 percent of everything they contribute to the account. If they try to contribute to the account behind your back, immediately take half of the account's worth and garnish your child's wages for the next few months.

See how fun financial education can be?

Tools to Help You Get Ahead

This section summarizes the many resources you've encountered throughout this book and adds a few more for extra help.

Banking and Credit Unions

Here are some resources to help you find a better bank or credit union and save on checks.

- Checks In The Mail, 800-733-4443, sells cheap checks.
- Credit Union National Association, 800-358-5710, will help you find a credit union in your area that you are qualified to join.
- Current, 800-204-2244, sells cheap checks.

Books

If you want more worksheets to take control of your budget, have I got a book for you. *The Budget Kit* by Judy Lawrence provides every worksheet you'll ever need. Another book worth having is the *Wholesale by Mail Catalog*. It lists catalogs of all types that will save you money. Finally, buy your new books at Amazon.com to save money or buy your books at used bookstores.

- *The Budget Kit,* Judy Lawrence, Dearborn Financial Publishing
- *Wholesale by Mail Catalog,* Prudence McCullough, HarperCollins
- Amazon.com, www.amazon.com. Sells new books online at a discount

Buying a Home

Here is a resource to help you decide whether to buy a home, then to help you get the most for your money.

- Fannie Mae (Federal National Mortgage Association), 800-732-6643, offers mortgage information and helpful literature on buying a home.

Community Organizations

Joining a community organization will not only introduce you to new friends, it will expand your ability to get better deals. Do business with your friends and family. They will treat you right, they will charge a fair price, and everybody will be happy. Contact the organizations below and check your phone book for a chapter near you. Also, check your church or synagogue for groups that you might enjoy.

- Elks, 773-477-2750, www.elks.org
- Kiwanis, 800-549-2647, www.kiwanis.org
- Rotary, www.rotary.org
- Toastmasters, 714-858-8255, www.toastmasters.org

Credit Cards

Throw out all department store cards. Keep no more than two major credit cards. Make sure they charge no annual fee. Pay your balance in full every month. Here are two places that will supply you with a list of no-fee cards.

- Bankcard Holders of America, 524 Branch Drive, Salem, VA 24153, 703-389-5445. No-fee credit card list is $4.
- RAM Research CardTrak, PO Box 1700, Frederick, MD 21702, 301-695-4660, www.ramresearch.com. No-fee credit card list is $5.

Credit Reports

You can check your own credit at any time. Send either of these companies a check for $9 and they'll send your credit report within thirty days. Because plans change frequently, call each company for details before sending money.

- Equifax Information Service Center, P.O. Box 740241, Atlanta, GA 30374-0241, 800-685-1111
- Experian National Consumer Assistance Center, P.O. Box 2104, Allen, TX 75013-2104, 888-397-3742

Debt

Getting out of debt should be one of your highest priorities. Here are resources to help you.

- Consumer Credit Counseling Service, 800-388-2227, provides low-cost debt counseling.
- Debt Counselors of America, www.dca.org, is a nonprofit resource for getting out of debt.
- National Center for Financial Education, P.O. Box 34070, San Diego, CA 92163. Send a self-addressed stamped ($1 rate) envelope for free brochures on how to live debt-free.

Discount Brokerage Firms

Discount brokerage firms will be important allies in your quest for financial prosperity. They are superb for consolidating your mutual fund portfolio and also provide an affordable way to buy and sell stocks.

Free Mutual Fund Trading, Fairly Cheap Stock Trading

- Charles Schwab & Company, 800-435-4000, www.schwab.com. Ask for information on OneSource, Schwab's no-load, no transaction fee network of mutual funds.
- Fidelity Investments, 800-544-8888, www.fidelity.com. Ask for information on FundsNetwork, Fidelity's no-load, no transaction fee network of mutual funds.

Dirt Cheap Stock Trading

- Ameritrade, www.ameritrade.com. Low-commission stock trading.
- Datek, www.datek.com. Low-commission stock trading.
- E*Trade, www.etrade.com. Low-commission stock trading.

Insurance

Buy only the insurance you need. Buy it as cheaply as possible. Here are the companies you should contact first. Always compare quotes from these companies to quotes from local companies in your phone book.

- Amica, 800-992-6422. The cheapest auto insurance I've found.
- Colonial Penn, 800-847-1729. Cheap auto insurance.
- Geico, 800-841-3000. Cheap policies of all kinds.
- Quotesmith, 800-431-1147. Lists best term life insurance policies from several companies.
- SelectQuote, 800-343-1985. Lists best life insurance policies from several companies.
- Termquote, 800-444-8376. Lists best insurance policies from several companies.
- 20th Century, 800-211-7233. Cheap insurance for California residents.
- USAA, 800-531-8080. Cheap insurance for active-duty and retired military officers and their dependents.
- Wholesale Insurance Network, 800-808-5810. Lists best insurance policies from several companies.

Long-distance Phone Companies

Call each of these companies to see which flat-rate long-distance plan is best for you. They can usually switch you right over the phone. You want a no-fee plan with a per-minute rate of 10 cents or less. Work with the numbers. If you find a low-fee plan with a lower per-minute charge, it might save you more money. You'll only have to do this shopping once, but the savings will extend over many years of dialing long distance.

- AT&T, 888-928-8932.
- Excel, 800-875-9235.
- Sprint, 800-877-4646.
- WorldCom, 888-926-6496.

Mail-order Companies

Call these companies to request free catalogs. Compare prices from the catalogs with specials advertised in your newspaper. By ordering from a few catalogs, your name will appear on mailing lists to receive competing catalogs. You'll quickly fill your home with easy ways to hunt for bargains.

- Damark, 800-729-9000. Home electronics.
- Dell Computer, 800-999-3355, www.dell.com. Computer equipment.
- Diversified Prescription Delivery, 800-452-1976. Prescription drugs.
- Gateway, 800-846-4208, www.gw2k.com. Computer equipment.
- Medi-Mail, 800-922-3444. Prescription drugs.
- Micron, 800-209-9686, www.micron.com. Computer equipment.

Neatest Little Publications

To get the most from this neatest little approach to managing your money, you need to be able to invest the difference between what you earn and what you spend. Investing will build your wealth. To do it right, read my books on mutual fund investing and stock market investing, then consider subscribing to my newsletters. Also, visit my Web site at www. neatmoney.com.

- *The Neatest Little Guide to Mutual Fund Investing* by Jason Kelly.
- *The Neatest Little Guide to Stock Market Investing* by Jason Kelly.
- *The Neatest Little FundLetter,* $75, 800-339-5671. My mutual fund newsletter shows ten real-life portfolios that you choose based on your time frame and amount of money to invest. Also lists my favorite funds in each

category with a complete list of performance figures, risk measurements, and toll-free phone numbers. Published monthly.

- *The NeatSheet,* $75, 800-339-5671. My stock newsletter tracks a real-life portfolio of five to twenty stocks. Also lists the stocks I'm watching and offers monthly advice on where to invest your regular monthly contribution.

Personal Finance Software

Software provides an easy way to track your expenses, manage your investments, and prepare your taxes. The two best programs are Intuit Quicken and Microsoft Money. Both are excellent, but differ slightly in their approach.

Let Your Computer Help Manage Your Money

Quicken uses a tried-and-true checkbook register format. You enter your purchases just as you would in a real checkbook. But the math is done for you, and every transaction is placed into categories that you define. You can then print out charts showing exactly where your money goes. Beyond those basics, the program offers online investment tracking, online banking, expert advice, and the ability to print checks instead of hand-writing them.

Microsoft Money recently deviated from the checkbook register format to a more contemporary hi-tech format. It's very sleek but a tad more difficult for first-time users to understand. You still enter transactions and they're still tallied for you in categories and charts. The program also offers online everything and the ability to print checks.

Both programs handle taxes well, but the edge goes to Quicken. Because Intuit also publishes TurboTax, the leading tax preparation software, you can use both products together seamlessly. You can edit your Quicken transactions from within TurboTax as you prepare your return. That's a cool feature, one that I find handy every year. Using Microsoft Money, you can export your tax information to a preparation program, but you can't edit the data directly in Money once you've exported.

While you won't go wrong with either Quicken or Money, I find Quicken to be the better of the two. It's the easiest to use, boasts an attractive interface, works best with tax software, and continues to be the industry leader.

- Intuit Quicken and TurboTax, www.intuit.com; also available in stores. Intuit publishes my favorite personal finance software.
- Microsoft Money, www.microsoft.com/money; also available in stores. An alternative to Quicken that uses a sleek, hi-tech interface.

Student Loans

Borrowing money for school launches too many people into a lifetime of debt. While an education is one of the best investments, you should still save money where possible. Here are some organizations to help.

- fastWEB, www.fastweb.com. Creates a student profile and searches more than 180,000 scholarships for free. With enough scholarships, you can avoid student loans entirely.
- Federal Direct Consolidation Loan, 800-4FED-AID. Combines student loans into a big loan with a low rate. The interest rate is variable, so the payment due will fluctuate from time to time.
- Sallie Mae (Student Loan Marketing Association), 800-643-0040. Offers several consolidation plans that will allow you to reduce your payments, lower your interest, or both. Rewards you with a lower rate for establishing automatic deductions from your bank account.

Superstores and Wholesale

Buying in bulk can save you lots of money. Make sure you can use the products you buy before they spoil. Call the numbers below for the location of a superstore near you.

- Costco, 800-774-2678, www.costco.com.
- Sam's Club, 888-746-7726, www.samsclub.com.

10 / Aloha!

 Aloha is how the Hawaiians say good-bye. It's also how they say hello. The word conjures images of tropical shores and a feeling of prosperity.

It's fitting that we conclude our journey together with the word aloha. We are saying good-bye, but you are saying hello to a prosperous future. As you think back over the contents of this book, you'll see that there is nothing difficult about it. Your lifelong strategy for financial comfort is this:

Spend less than you earn, invest the difference, and protect what you have.

The details change a bit from person to person, issue to issue, and even age to age. But the spirit of prosperity will always be captured by that strategy. You will never go wrong by living within your means. Perfect it, enjoy your life, and teach your children the same kind of success.

Drop me a line sometime. You can E-mail me directly, jkelly@neatmoney.com, or stop by www.neatmoney.com to send me a message from there.

There's one last thing you need to do for me. Set the book down, look out the window, and say "There really is a better way. I've finally found it. I'm going to use it."

Aloha!

Net Worth Worksheet

Current Assets

Cash on hand _____
Checking accounts _____
Savings accounts _____
Short-term bank CDs _____
Money market accounts _____
Other _____
TOTAL CURRENT ASSETS _____

Investment Assets

401(k) or 403(b) plans _____
Annuities _____
IRAs _____
Other retirement plans _____
Long-term CDs _____
Stocks _____
Stock mutual funds _____
Bonds _____
Bond mutual funds _____
Other _____
TOTAL INVESTMENT ASSETS _____

Personal Property

Automobiles _____
Recreational vehicles _____
Home furnishings _____
Collectibles _____
Artwork _____
Jewelry _____
Other _____
TOTAL PERSONAL PROPERTY _____

Real Estate

Primary residence _____
Vacation home _____
Rental property _____
Land _____
Other _____
TOTAL REAL ESTATE _____

Total Assets

TOTAL ASSETS _____

Current Liabilities

Department store credit cards _____

Major credit cards _____

Medical and dental bills _____

Other _____

TOTAL CURRENT LIABILITIES [_____]

Loans

Automobile loans _____

Educational loans _____

Personal loans _____

Installment contracts _____

Home equity loans _____

Other _____

TOTAL LOANS [_____]

Mortgages

Primary residence _____

Vacation home _____

Rental property _____

Other _____

TOTAL MORTGAGES [_____]

Total Liabilities

TOTAL LIABILITIES [_____]

Net Worth

Total Assets _____

minus Total Liabilities _____

NET WORTH [_____]

Monthly Expenses

Month: Year:

Categories										Totals
Taxes										
Mortgage or Rent										
Credit Card Interest										
Automobile, Gasoline										
Groceries										
Dining Out, Snacks										
Natural Gas										
Electricity										
Water										
Garbage, Sewer										
Telephone										
Cable Television										
Auto Insurance										
Homeowner's Insurance										
Life Insurance										
Disability Insurance										
Medical Insurance										
Doctor Visits										
Prescriptions										
Clothing Purchase										

Categories							Totals
Cosmetics							
Toiletries							
Hair Care							
Books, Magazines							
Movies							
Computer Hardware							
Computer Software							
Laundry							
Childcare							
Gifts							
Entertainment							
Vacations							
Sports, Recreation							
Music, CDs, Tapes							
Kitchen Appliances							
Office Equipment							
Home Electronics							
Education							
Pet, Veterinary, Food							
Charity							
Professional Services							
Other Expenses							

Monthly Total:

Yearly Expenses

Year:

Categories	Jan	Feb	Mar	Apr	May	Jun	Jul	Aug	Sep	Oct	Nov	Dec	Totals
Taxes													
Mortgage or Rent													
Credit Card Interest													
Automobile, Gasoline													
Groceries													
Dining Out, Snacks													
Natural Gas													
Electricity													
Water													
Garbage, Sewer													
Telephone													
Cable Television													
Auto Insurance													
Homeowner's Insurance													
Life Insurance													
Disability Insurance													
Medical Insurance													
Doctor Visits													
Prescriptions													
Clothing Purchase													
Cosmetics													
Toiletries													

Hair Care																			
Books, Magazines																			
Movies																			
Computer Hardware																			
Computer Software																			
Laundry																			
Childcare																			
Gifts																			
Entertainment																			
Vacations																			
Sports, Recreation																			
Music, CDs, Tapes																			
Kitchen Appliances																			
Office Equipment																			
Home Electronics																			
Education																			
Pet, Veterinary, Food																			
Charity																			
Professional Services																			
Other Expenses																			
Monthly Totals:																			